SOLDIER'S HANDBOOK FOR DEFENSE AGAINST CHEMICAL AND BIOLOGICAL OPERATIONS AND NUCLEAR WARFARE

Fredonia Books
Amsterdam, The Netherlands

Soldier's Handbook for Defense Against Chemical
and Biological Operations and Nuclear Warfare

by
U. S. Department of the Army

ISBN: 1-58963-543-4

Copyright © 2001 by Fredonia Books

Reprinted from the 1967 edition

Fredonia Books
Amsterdam, the Netherlands
http://www.fredoniabooks.com

FIELD MANUAL ⎱
No. 21-41 ⎰

HEADQUARTERS
DEPARTMENT OF THE ARMY
Washington, D. C., *6 February 1967*

SOLDIER'S HANDBOOK FOR DEFENSE AGAINST CHEMICAL AND BIOLOGICAL OPERATIONS AND NUCLEAR WARFARE

———

———

* This manual supersedes FM 21–41, 23 April 1963, including C 1, 10 April 1964.

CHAPTER 1

INTRODUCTION

Section I. GENERAL

1. Purpose and Scope

a. This manual provides the soldier with procedures for individual defensive measures against chemical and biological operations and nuclear warfare. It also provides guidance for company commanders and platoon, section, and squad leaders for the accomplishment of individual training in defense against chemical, biological, and nuclear attack.

b. Selected information conforms to agreements between the United States and certain allied countries. Details of information on alarm systems, marking of contaminated areas, and a new color system for the automatic atropine injector are based on such agreements. The documents which formalized these agreements are called Standardization Agreements (STANAGS) and are listed in appendix I.

c. The material contained herein is applicable to both nuclear and nonnuclear warfare.

2. Organization

This manual is divided into four chapters, with three appendixes. Chapter 1 is introductory in nature; section I contains general information, section II includes broad information applicable to individual protection, and section III describes the field protective mask and gives instructions for its use. Chapter 2 covers individual protective procedures in chemical operations, chapter 3 covers individual protective procedures in biological operations, and chapter 4 covers individual protective procedures in nuclear warfare. Each of these chapters is divided into three sections. The organization is parallel so that section I of each chapter covers those things a soldier must learn before an attack occurs in order for him to be able to minimize the effects, section II covers those things he must do during an attack, and section III covers those things he must do after an attack. Appendix I is a list of references; appendix II describes individual proficiency standards; and appendix III outlines procedures for inspection and fitting of the field protective mask, carrying positions, and mask drill.

3. Definitions

Definitions of terms used in this manual are in AR 320–5.

4. Changes

Users of this manual are encouraged to submit recommended changes and comments to improve the manual. Comments should be keyed to the specific page, paragraph, and line of the text in which change is recommended. Reasons should be provided for each comment to insure understanding and complete evaluation. Comments should be forwarded direct to Commandant, U.S. Army

Chemical Center and School, Fort McClellan, Ala. 36201.

Section II. YOUR INDIVIDUAL RESPONSIBILITIES

5. You Must Be Able to Protect Yourself

a. This manual is for you, the individual soldier. Its purpose is to help you accomplish your mission and live to tell about it if chemical or biological agents or nuclear weapons are used against you.

b. When any poison gets into your body, it can cause sickness or death. Likewise, when chemical, biological, or nuclear attacks occur, some casualties are possible. Casualties are soldiers put out of action—sick, wounded, missing, or killed. Chemical agents, biological agents, and nuclear explosions cause casualties just as bullets and high explosives do. However, the number of casualties will depend on the actions of *the individual soldier.* You have learned the actions to take for protection against gunfire and bombs. Learning the actions to take for protection against chemical and biological agents and nuclear explosions is just as important. As you go through this manual, you will find that you have a very effective means for protection against chemical and biological agents: your field protective mask. Protection against the effects of nuclear explosions is possible primarily through actions taken to shield yourself. Learn *now* what you must do to protect yourself and to help maintain the combat efficiency of your unit.

6. Why This Manual Was Written

This manual was written to assist you in learning basic facts that you must know to avoid becoming a casualty in the event of chemical, biological, or nuclear attack and accomplish your mission. It will answer most of your questions about defense against these attacks. Your unit CBR-trained personnel will give you additional information and training.

7. How To Get the Most From This Manual

As you study this manual, keep in mind that the mission must be accomplished, but ask yourself the following questions:

a. What are chemical operations? Biological operations? What is nuclear warfare?

b. How can chemical agents, biological agents, and nuclear explosions injure or kill me?

c. How may I be attacked?

d. How will I know when an attack occurs?

e. What can I do before an attack to minimize the effects?

f. What can I do during an attack to minimize the effects?

g. What can I do after an attack to minimize the effects?

h. What can I do to minimize the number of casualties in my unit?

The facts which answer these questions for you are in this manual. Remember them! They can save your life!

8. Many Threats

In the past a soldier was trained to defend against the hazards of chemical agents and high-

CHEMICAL OPERATIONS
THE EMPLOYMENT OF CHEMICAL AGENTS (EXCLUDING RIOT CONTROL AGENTS) TO: (1) KILL OR INCAPACITATE FOR A SIGNIFICANT PERIOD OF TIME, MAN OR ANIMALS (2) DENY OR HINDER THE USE OF SPACE, FACILITIES, OR MATERIAL.
BIOLOGICAL OPERATIONS
THE EMPLOYMENT OF BIOLOGICAL AGENTS IN A WEAPON SYSTEM TO PRODUCE CASUALTIES OR DAMAGE
NUCLEAR WARFARE
THE EMPLOYMENT OF NUCLEAR WEAPONS TO PRODUCE CASUALTIES OR CAUSE DESTRUCTION

Figure 1. Chemical and biological operations and nuclear warfare defined.

explosive weapons. Today, in addition to these, he also must be prepared to defend against the hazards of biological agents and nuclear weapons. Chemical and biological operations are not separate forms of warfare; hence, they may be part of either a nuclear or nonnuclear war. Chemical operations, biological operations, and nuclear warfare are defined in figure 1.

9. Chemical and Biological Operations and Nuclear Warfare

a. General. The primary purpose of chemical operations, biological operations, and nuclear warfare is to produce casualties in man and animals and to deny or hinder the use of space, facilities, or material.

b. Chemical Operations (fig. 1). Chemical agents used in chemical operations are similar to poisonous compounds with which we are familiar in everyday life. Carbon monoxide gas escaping from your automobile exhaust can kill if a sufficient amount is inhaled. You probably have used chemical compounds to kill flies, mosquitoes, and other insects. Chemical agents, however, are much more powerful; and they are released to cover relatively large areas. Chemical agents can be placed on your position as vapor (gas), as finely divided liquid or solid particles (aerosols), or as liquid droplets. Vapors and aerosols are not likely to be visible; however, liquid droplets may have the appearance of drops of rain or dew. These agents are likely to be odorless and to have little or no color. The enemy may even use a mixture of agents, hoping to cause confusion and thus to increase casualties.

c. *Biological Operations* (fig. 1). Biological agents used in biological operations are the same disease-producing microorganisms (germs) naturally present around us every day. Some of these microorganisms cause such diseases as measles, flu, and chickenpox. You know that diseases are caused by living organisms too small for you to set unless you use a microscope. The intentional use of microorganisms makes biological operations different from natural disease hazards. Many microorganisms are harmless, and most are actually helpful to us. Only a few of the disease-producing microorganisms are harmful enough to be used as biological agents. Man's fight against disease-producing microorganisms is not new; it started the moment he was born. Immunization (shots) are given to help the body increase its defenses against disease. One of the first things you did on becoming a soldier was to take immunizations to protect you from diseases such as typhoid fever, tetanus, and flu. During World War II, soldiers in the tropics were careful to take Atabrine to guard against malaria. Any belief that biological operations concern some unknown superweapon is not based on fact. Biological operations are simply a manmade attempt to produce disease.

d. *Nuclear Warfare* (fig. 1). Heat, blast, and nuclear radiation are the hazards found in nuclear warfare. These hazards are not new to you. The heat (thermal radiation) and blast effects of a nuclear explosion are similar to those of high explosives, but a nuclear explosion can be many times more powerful than the largest TNT bomb. Radiation is often used in the diagnosis and treatment of illnesses. X-rays are good examples and have been used for about 70 years. If they are not carefully controlled, however, sickness or death can result. Similarly, sickness and death can result from radiation produced by nuclear weapons.

10. Protection Against Chemical and Biological Agents and Nuclear Weapons

a. You must protect yourself from the effects of chemical and biological agents and nuclear explosions as you perform your mission. The use of correct individual defensive measures can protect you from many of the hazards; therefore, you must learn these measures so that you will not become a casualty and so that you may assist your unit in accomplishing its mission. As a well-trained soldier, you must be able to take the correct protective action, to correctively use your protective equipment, and to make the most of any available covering or shelter.

b. To protect yourself against the effects of chemical and biological agents, you need protective equipment and protective measures to block the entry of these agents into your body. These agents can enter your body through your—

(1) EYES.

(2) NOSE.

(3) MOUTH.

(4) SKIN.

You also must be able to protect yourself against the blast, heat, and initial and residual nuclear radiation caused by a nuclear explosion.

c. The dangers of chemical and biological operations and nuclear warfare may occur separately or together. The enemy will use any weapon or any combination of weapons that he thinks will put you and your unit out of action. This means that he may use a nuclear weapon and then follow up with a chemical attack. He may use chemical agents to contaminate certain areas in hopes of forcing your unit into a position more vulnerable for a nuclear attack. He may use biological agents to inflict casualties in hopes of lowering your unit's fighting power. Since different types of attacks may occur at the same time, or one type may immediately succeed another, you must be able to take all the measures required for protection against all hazards. Some of the measures for protection against chemical and biological agents are identical, and some are similar to those for protection against the effects of nuclear weapons. For example, your mask is your most important single item for protection against both chemical and biological agents. You will stop breathing and mask without order or alarm upon indication of either a chemical or biological attack, and you will wear your mask after either type of attack until ordered to unmask. If a nuclear attack follows immediately, you must take the added actions required for protection against it that are not required against either a chemical or biological attack. As you study, you must identify and understand which measures are the same for each type of attack.

d. To protect yourself against the effects of chemical and biological agents and nuclear radiation, you must know what areas are contaminated. Standard markers (fig. 2) are used to mark contaminated areas. Study these markers until you can easily recognize them. Remember, however, that contaminated areas may not be marked, and you must be alert for any indication of possible contamination.

(1) *Description.* The markers are right-angled isosceles triangles with a base of 28 centimeters (approximately 11½ inches) and sides of 20 centimeters (approximately 8 inches. The color of the marker and the word on the front indicate the type of contamination in an area. The words to be used are GAS for chemical, BIO for biological, and ATOM for radiological contamination. Information concerning the contamination will be added to the back of the marker. The identifying colors and words as well as the information to be placed on the back of each marker, are included in figure 2. The standard markers will be made of wood, metal, plastic, composition board, or other rigid material. If standard markers are not available, expedients containing the same information may be made of any suitable material.

CBR MARKERS

GAS

CHEMICAL
YELLOW BACKGROUND WITH RED
LETTERING

NAME OF AGENT (IF KNOWN)
DATE AND TIME OF DETECTION

28 CM
20 CM   20 CM

BIO

BIOLOGICAL
BLUE BACKGROUND WITH RED
LETTERING

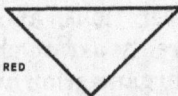
NAME OF AGENT (IF KNOWN)
DATE AND TIME OF DETECTION

ATOM

RADIOLOGICAL
WHITE BACKGROUND WITH BLACK
LETTERING

DOSE RATE
DATE AND TIME OF READING
DATE AND TIME OF BURST
(IF KNOWN)

SURFACE OF MARKER FACING
AWAY FROM CONTAMINATION
(FRONT)

SURFACE OF MARKER FACING
CONTAMINATION
(BACK)

CHEMICAL MINEFIELD
(UNEXPLODED MINES)

GAS MINES

RED BACKGROUND WITH YELLOW
LETTERING AND STRIPE

CHEMICAL AGENT IN MINE
DATE OF EMPLACEMENT

SURFACE OF MARKER FACING
AWAY FROM MINEFIELD
(FRONT)

SURFACE OF MARKER FACING
MINEFIELD
(BACK)

*Figure 2. Markers for contaminated or
dangerous land areas.*

(2) *Use.* The markers will be placed above the ground on wires, trees, or rocks with the right-angled point downward, and the front facing away from the contaminated area. When you see the word GAS, BIO, or ATOM, you are outside the contaminated area. Where more than one kind of contamination is in an area, the appropriate markers will be used near each other.

e. The subjects of chemical operations, biological operations, and nuclear warfare are treated in three separate chapters in this manual because this organization will make it easier for you to use the manual. In a combat situation, the dangers you face and the actions you must take cannot be tied into three such neat packages. Learn now how to protect yourself against *all* the weapons of modern warfare. Stay constantly alert to any indication that the enemy has used a chemical agent, a biological agent, or a nuclear weapon.

11. Your Field Protective Mask

Your field protective mask will be one of your best friends during situations where chemical or biological agents are used against you. It will protect your face, eyes, and respiratory tract from field concentrations of chemical and biological agents. You must care for your mask just as you care for your individual weapon. After all, both of them can save your life. In addition to your mask, you will be issued certain accessories. Paragraphs 20 through 27 describe your mask and its accessories and give you instructions for donning, wearing, and caring for the mask. Appendix III includes instructions for mask inspection and fitting, illustrations of mask drill commands and carrying positions, and information on what to do with your helmet, weapon, and eyeglasses while you are donning your mask. Your unit leaders will conduct training in donning, wearing, and caring for your mask. They will also conduct inspections and mask drill. Conditions for automatic masking without order or alarm (para 45, 71) are illustrated in outline form in figure 8. Instructions for unmasking after a chemical attack are covered in paragraph 42 and after a biological attack in paragraph 71. Use these references to aid you in becoming and remaining proficient in using and caring for your mask.

12. Protective Clothing and Covering

Use the protective clothing and any covering available to you to protect yourself against chemical and biological agents and the effects of nuclear weapons.

13. Care of Your Equipment

The Army is constantly developing and testing new and better types of protective equipment. The American soldier will be well equipped and trained to meet any form of chemical, biological, or nuclear attack. Regardless of how much money and time are spent to give you the best possible protection, one factor is your responsibility. *You are responsible for the proper care of all protective equipment issued to you.* If you fail to take this responsibility seriously, it may result in your becoming a casualty and in success for the enemy.

14. First Aid Is Vital

During your basic training you learned that first aid is a skill every soldier must have. Now, more than ever, you must know those measures which can save your life and the lives of others. If you have not received prior training in first aid for chemical agents, it may seem difficult to remember or difficult to do. First aid for injuries from nuclear explosions is the same as for injuries from other types of explosions. Your unit officers and NCO's will give first-aid training. This manual will help you to get first-aid measures firmly fixed in your mind. You must be able to rely on *yourself* when first aid is required. Remember that the aidman may be a casualty and be unable to help you.

15. Harmful Agents Can Be Neutralized and Radioactive Particles Removed

It is possible to make harmful chemical and biological agents lose their harmful effects and to remove radiological contamination by procedures referred to as *decontamination*. In some cases, especially involving chemical agents, decontamination and first-aid measures are very closely related and may even overlap. Details of how you can accomplish decontamination are covered in chapters 2 through 4. The knowledge that the effects of harmful agents and nuclear radiation can be minimized will build confidence in your ability to continue your mission in their presence.

16. Alarm Systems

Two types of CBR alarm systems may be used to alert you in the event of chemical, biological, or nuclear attack (fig. 3).

a. General Alarm. The general alarm will be spread by normal means of communication, such as telephone and radio, when an attack is expected over a large area.

b. Local Alarm. Your unit SOP sets forth how and when local alarms will be given. The prescribed method for spreading such alarm is the rapid and continuous striking of percussion devices that will make an easily recognized sound. Objects that may be used include bells, metal triangles, iron rails, iron pipes, and empty shell cases. As a supplement to these alarms, or to replace them when the tactical situation does not permit their use, certain visual signals are used to give emergency warning of an attack. The signals consist of donning the mask and protective equipment, followed by any exaggerated motions to call attention to this fact. In the event of a chemical attack, there is danger of breathing in the agent if you give a vocal alarm before masking; therefore, *you should mask first,* then give the alarm. Shout SPRAY for a spray attack and GAS for an attack delivered by other means. The vocal alarm is to warn those close to you and does not take the place of the percussion-type alarm to alert a unit of a chemical attack. Remember that other alarms such as the air raid siren may be heard first, followed by the percussion alarm,

GENERAL ALARM FOR EXPECTED ATTACK

TELEPHONE   FIELD RADIO

LOCAL ALARM FOR DETECTED ATTACK

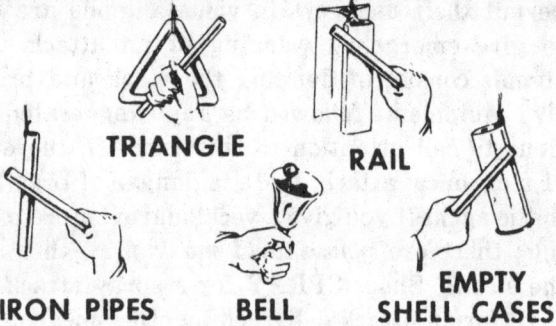

TRIANGLE

RAIL

IRON PIPES   BELL   EMPTY SHELL CASES

ANY CONVENIENT PERCUSSION
ALARM AS SPECIFIED IN UNIT SOP

*Figure 3. Alarm systems for chemical, biological,
or nuclear attack.*

AGO 6631C

EVERY SOLDIER MUST **KNOW**:

1. THE CHARACTERISTICS AND EFFECTS OF CHEMICAL AND BIOLOGICAL AGENTS AND NUCLEAR EXPLOSIONS

2. HOW TO RECOGNIZE AND PROTECT HIMSELF AGAINST CHEMICAL, BIOLOGICAL, AND NUCLEAR ATTACKS

3. HOW TO PERFORM FIRST AID FOR CASUALTIES CAUSED BY CHEMICAL AND NUCLEAR ATTACKS.

4. HOW TO REMOVE CHEMICAL AND BIOLOGICAL AGENTS AND RADIOACTIVE PARTICLES FROM HIMSELF AND HIS EQUIPMENT.

5. THE PROCEDURES FOR MASKING

6. THE CONDITIONS FOR MASKING WITHOUT ALARM OR COMMAND.

7. THE PROCEDURES FOR UNMASKING.

Figure 4. Training objectives.

to indicate an actual or suspected chemical, biological, or nuclear attack.

17. Your Objectives

You must master seven basic objectives. These objectives are listed in figure 4. Learning what these objectives are now will make the chapters to follow easier to understand and will increase your ability to master the minimum standards of proficiency which are covered in appendix II.

18. Be Prepared

Evidence points toward the strong possibility that our potential enemies have the capability to use chemical and biological agents and nuclear weapons against us. We cannot afford to disregard this capability. You must master the basic protective measures given in this manual while there is still time.

19. Successful Accomplishment of the Mission

When you have mastered the seven objectives listed in figure 4, the results will justify your efforts. You and your unit will then be prepared to perform assigned missions against an enemy using chemical agents, biological agents, or nuclear weapons. Successful mission accomplishment will be the result of training. Knowledge, confidence, and courage will replace fear and panic.

Section III. YOUR FIELD PROTECTIVE MASK

20. The Value of Your Field Protective Mask

a. Your mask is the most important single item of protective equipment you have against chemical and biological agents. In World Wars I and II it was known simply as a gas mask. Today, it is called a protective mask because it protects you against inhaling chemical and biological agents and it can be used following a nuclear attack where sufficient dust is present in the air to make breathing difficult. The protective mask does not protect against industrial gases and ammonia.

b. To avoid becoming a casualty in chemical or biological operations, you must keep agents from getting on or entering your body. While the protective mask alone cannot do this, it does play the major role. It prevents you from inhaling and from getting into your eyes and mouth all known chemical and biological agents.

21. How Your Protective Mask Works

Your protective mask contains two filter elements which trap chemical and biological agents in vapor and aerosol form. When you wear a mask, you draw air into it by inhaling. This air is purified by the filter elements before it enters your nose or mouth. The ABC–M17 field protective mask is the standard A field protective mask. If you are assigned to certain units, such as aviation or tank companies, you may be issued a different type of mask which will afford you the same protection as the ABC–M17 mask. See appendix I for publications which give details on such masks.

a. The ABC–M17 Field Protective Mask (fig. 5). The filter system of the ABC–M17 mask consists of two filter elements contained in pouches

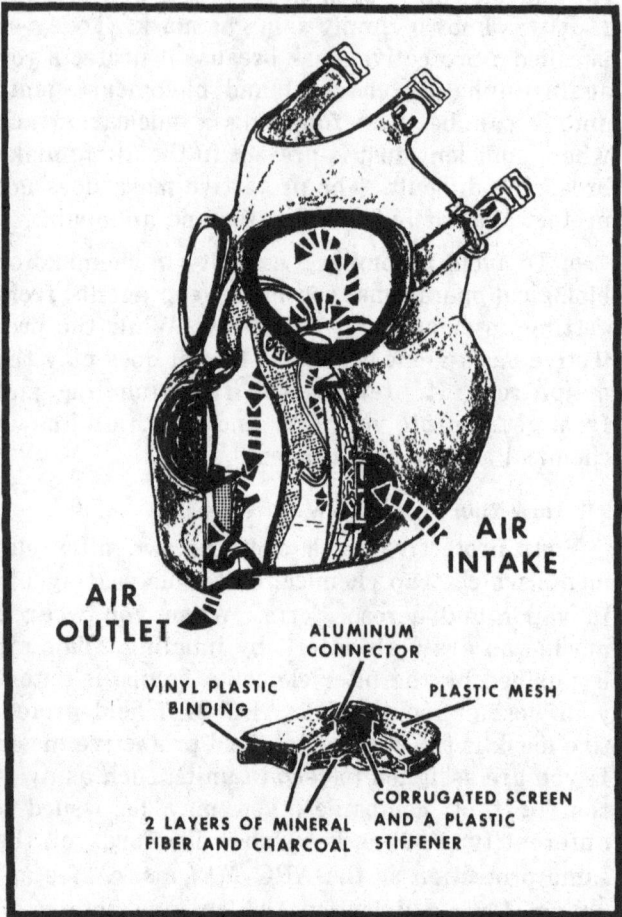

AIR
INTAKE

AIR
OUTLET

ALUMINUM
CONNECTOR

VINYL PLASTIC
BINDING

PLASTIC MESH

CORRUGATED SCREEN
AND A PLASTIC
STIFFENER

2 LAYERS OF MINERAL
FIBER AND CHARCOAL

Figure 5. Airflow through the ABC–M17 field protective
mask and a sectional view of filter element.

molded in the cheeks of the facepiece. These filter elements, or filter pads, are both mechanical and chemical purifiers. Each filter element consists of two layers of mineral fiber and charcoal. Air is inhaled through two inlet valves, located on the outer surface of each cheek pouch. The incoming filtered air passes from the cheek pouches through deflector tubes which direct the air across the eyelenses, keeping them free of condensation. The filtered air then passes through two one-way valves, one in each side of the nosecup. Breathing may be either through the nose or through the mouth. Exhaled air is discharged through an outlet valve at the chin position. The M17 mask assembly includes the facepiece assembly, the carrier, and two eyelens outserts. The two eyelens outserts are provided for attachment over the mask eyelenses. In very cold regions, the outserts prevent fogging of the eyelenses, caused by condensation of exhaled breath. The outserts should be worn at all times to protect the eyelenses from becoming damaged. You can communicate understandably through the voicemitter-outlet valve assembly. The mask carrier (fig. 23) is designed with pockets to hold the accessories issued with the mask (*b* below). The fastened flap of the carrier is positioned vertically against the body.

b. Accessories for the ABC–M17 Field Protective Mask (fig. 6).

(1) *M5A4 protection and treatment set or M13 individual decontaminating and reimpregnating kit.* You may be issued either the protection and treatment set

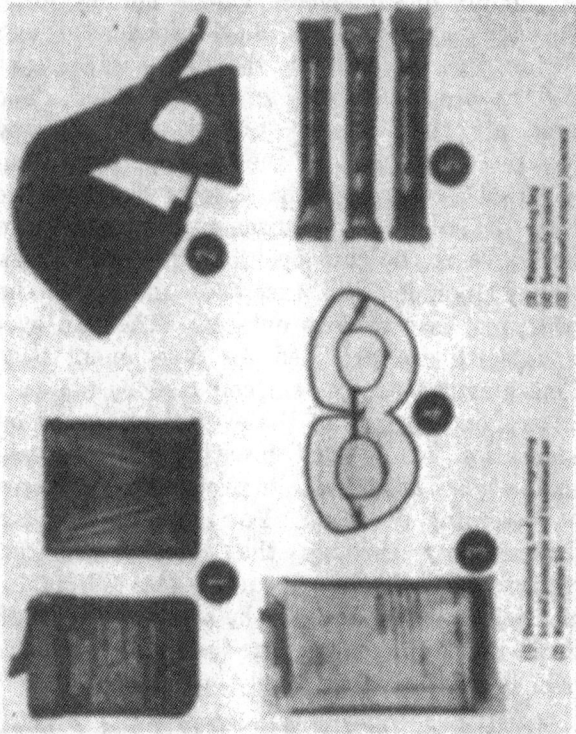

Figure 6. Accessories for the ABC–M17 field protective mask.

Figure 6—Continued.

or the individual decontaminating and reimpregnating kit. The protection and treatment set contains four tubes of protective ointment and absorbent clothes to be used primarily for decontaminating chemical agents on the skin; the set may be used for decontaminating individual equipment in an emergency. Use of the ointment is discussed in paragraph 40*c*-(1). The M13 individual decontaminating and reimpregnating kit contains two cloth bags filled with powder for use either in decontaminating individual clothing and equipment or reimpregnating the chemical protective liner, gloves, and socks. It also contains a small pad filled with skin decontaminating powder, and a single-edge cutter blade. Use of the kit is discussed in paragraph 40*c*(2). The M5A4 set of the M13 kit, whichever you are issued, will be stored in the bottom rear pocket of the mask carrier.

(2) *M4 mask winterization kit*. The mask winterization kit is used with the protective mask in extremely cold weather to prevent frost accumulations which will cause the mask to malfunction. It will also give some protection against frostbite of the face. If issued, it may be stored while attached to the mask in the carrier; when not in use, it is stored in the inside pocket of the mask carrier.

(3) *M1 waterproofing bag*. The plastic waterproofing bag is designed to protect the filter elements against dampness. The mask is placed in the bag which is then secured at the top with rubber bands provided. The mask, in the plastic bag, is placed back into the carrier. Since moisture forms on the inside of the plastic bag, the mask should be removed

from the bag every 24 hours and both dried out. When not in use, the waterproofing bag is stored in the bottom rear pocket of the mask carrier.

(4) *Spectacle inserts.* Spectacle inserts are available, by prescription of the medical officer in charge, for personnel who must wear glasses with the mask. The spectacles are designed to fit as inserts into the eyepieces of the mask. The inserts will be taken with you when you transfer.

(5) *Automatic atropine injectors.* Automatic atropine injectors are used in the treatment of nerve agent poisoning. When issued, the three automatic injectors will be carried in the top rear pocket of the mask carrier. Use of the injectors is covered in paragraph 49.

(6) *M6A2 protective mask hood.* The mask hood protects the head, neck, and shoulders from contamination and increases protection to the respiratory tract by minimizing the effects of leakage around the edges of the mask. It will prevent contamination of the mask by liquid agent, minimizing decontamination procedures. The hood may be stored attached to the mask in the carrier.

22. Fitting and Adjusting Your Mask

a. You know that chemical agents are very dangerous. Biological agents are equally dangerous even though they do not cause immediate irritation and do not produce immediate symptoms. For you to stop breathing and mask upon suspicion of a chemical or biological attack is not enough to keep these agents out of your body. *Your mask must fit your head and face so that it will be airtight when you have properly donned it.*

b. There are three sizes of protective masks: small, medium, and large. The size of your mask should be checked at time of issue, and the mask must be fitted and adjusted (app III). Correct adjustment prevents leakage, temple pressure, and general discomfort. Many soldiers make the mistake of pulling the straps too tight. Correct adjustment does not mean an extremely tight fit, but rather a close fit. Pay close attention to how your mask is checked for proper adjustment, because the time may come when adjustment will be up to you alone.

23. Speed in Putting on Your Mask Versus an Airtight Seal

You may ask which is more important: speed in putting on the mask or getting an airtight seal. Both are absolutely necessary. Learning how to get an airtight seal is stressed in early training. This is correct procedure, since speed in masking at the expense of a good seal can result in inhaling agents. After you have been drilled in the masking procedure until you do it automatically, you work for speed. To be well trained, you must become expert both in putting on your mask and in getting an airtight seal in 9 seconds or less.

24. How to Don Your Mask

a. You know that, in your everyday life, doing certain things in the same way every time saves you much time and effort. One reason you can tear down and assemble your weapon in the dark is that you go through a series of actions in a set order. This idea also applies to putting on your mask. Donning your protective mask is no more complicated than putting on your headgear if you always go through the proper motions in the proper order.

b. The purpose of protective mask drill is to teach you exactly how to don, check, and remove the mask. The following reminders will help you remember the correct procedures:

(1) Be sure that you know the authorized positions for carrying the mask. The amount and kind of equipment you must carry will change from time to time. If you know all the carrying positions for the mask, you can select one that will enable you to easily reach it, regardless of other equipment that you must carry. Appendix III gives instructions for assuming the carrying positions and figure 25 illustrates the positions.

(2) Be sure that your mask carrier is positioned with the carrier flap toward your body. You can then open the carrier quickly with your left hand, leaving your right hand free for removing your headgear and taking the mask out of the car-

rier. Do not drop or place your headgear on the ground where it may become contaminated. Instructions for handling your headgear are in section III, appendix III.

(3) When removing your mask from the carrier, always grasp it in the area below the eyepieces. Remember that dirty handprints on the eyepieces will interfere with your vision and will only have to be removed. Never remove the mask from the carrier by pulling on the outlet valve cover.

(4) To put on your mask, grasp the facepiece with both hands and slide your thumbs inside so that the facepiece is opened to the fullest extent. Grasping the head harness tends to pull the edges together, which makes it very difficult to get the mask over your face.

(5) Place your chin in the chin pocket and pull the head harness over your head. Be sure all head straps are straight and the head pad is centered. If they are not, the mask will be uncomfortable, and you may not get a seal around the facepiece. Head straps can best be adjusted by a quick jerk or pull, rather than a steady pull.

(6) Use firm upward and outward strokes to smooth the edges of the facepiece and press them to your face.

(7) Always check your mask. To clear your mask, place the palm of one hand over the bottom of the outlet valve cover ((3a), fig. 26). Blow into the mask forceably with the air that is already in your lungs. Air escapes around the facepiece, forcing the contaminated air out. Then to test for leaks, place the palms of your hands over the two inlet valve assemblies in the cheek pouches to shut off air, and breathe in slowly ((3b), fig. 26). The facepiece will collapse against your face if there are no leaks. If the facepiece does not collapse, chances are that your head harness needs adjusting or that you do not have the mask properly positioned on your face. Any object that comes between your face and the edges of the facepiece can cause improper positioning. For example, your hair may fall down over your forehead and get between your mask and your face.

Note. You will not be able to test your mask for leaks by placing your hands in the manner described above if you are wearing cotton protective gloves. To test for leaks when wearing cotton protective gloves, fold the outside of your mask hood against the air inlet valve assemblies and press to shut off air.

(8) In unmasking, remove your headgear with your left hand, leaving the right hand free to remove the mask.

(9) To remove your mask, grasp the face-piece by the voicemitter-outlet valve assembly with the right hand. Remove the mask, using a downward, outward, then upward motion. Replace headgear.

(10) Take care to properly replace your mask in the carrier. This is well worth the few seconds it takes because you will save the time when you must remove the mask from the carrier. With your left hand, fold the head harness into the face-piece ((5b), fig. 26). Hold the carrier open with the left hand; hold the face-piece below the eyepiece with the right hand. Be sure to keep your hands off the eyepieces. Insert the mask in the carrier, chin pocket first and the eye-pieces facing downward. Then, tilt the mask upward so that the facepiece is facing outward ((6a), fig. 26). Close the carrier flap.

c. After learning the correct procedures for masking, you are trained to mask quickly and correctly under various field conditions (such as in darkness, in various types of uniforms, and with or without equipment) and in various positions (such as standing, prone, and kneeling). You are also trained in using additional protective measures necessitated by combat conditions; for example, shielding the inside of the mask facepiece, your headgear, and your weapon from liquid contamination.

25. Practice Wearing Your Mask

Although it may be inconvenient and slightly uncomfortable to wear your protective mask, the ease with which you can wear it for extended periods of time increases with practice and self-discipline. Much more important than complete comfort, however, are two other factors—that your life is safeguarded and that you are able to carry on with your mission during and after a chemical or biological attack. This means to fire your weapon, march, crawl, drive, or perform any other task assigned to you. You won't be able to do that unless you practice now. In spite of the fact that chemical or biological agents are used, the war will go on. Weapons must be fired. Foxholes must be dug. Messages must be sent. Trucks must move. Practice today may save your life tomorrow.

26. The Purpose of Protective Mask Drill

a. Drill in the proper procedures for putting on the protective mask is done to insure perfection. The steps that make up the drill have been carefully tested. These steps, when followed exactly, result in correct donning in a matter of seconds. Drill will also result in your being able to put on your mask automatically. You should do this as a reflex action without hesitation, just as a good driver puts on the brakes in an emergency. Appendix III illustrates the carrying positions and outlines procedures for donning and removing the mask. Your unit leaders will drill you in these procedures until you are able to mask automatically in 9 seconds or less.

b. This manual does not cover the tactics of chemical and biological operations and nuclear warfare. However, surprise is a big factor in the success of any attack, particularly one using chemical or biological agents. The enemy will be constantly trying to catch you off guard. Your surest defense against surprise is being able to mask correctly in a matter of seconds. Drill enables you to do this.

27. Care of Your Protective Mask Is Your Responsibility

a. You are responsible for the care of your protective mask. In view of the dangers of chemical and biological operations, you must take excellent care of your mask.

b. Water damages the filter elements of the M17 mask and destroys their efficiency. Use your waterproofing bag (para 21*b*(3)) to protect the filter elements against all dampness, including moisture from humidity.

c. Never lie or sit on your mask. A good soldier does not abuse his rifle. A good artilleryman does not let his fieldpiece be in any condition but the best. Regardless of the branch of service you are in, your protective mask is vital to your safety when chemical agents or biological agents are used. Treat your mask with the same respect that you treat your weapon or any other equipment which can save your life.

CHAPTER 2

PROCEDURES IN CHEMICAL OPERATIONS

Section I. THINGS TO DO BEFORE A CHEMICAL CHECK

28. General

The purpose of this chapter is to explain how chemical agents affect your body and to describe the individual actions that you must take to minimize the possibility of your becoming a casualty.

29. How the Enemy Can Attack You

Chemical agents can be disseminated by artillery fire, mortar fire, rockets, missiles, aircraft spray, bombs, grenades, and landmines. Other means of dissemination are possible. Always be alert because agents may already be on the ground or in the air.

30. Chemical Agents Defined

For the purposes of this manual, chemical agents are defined as substances in either gaseous, liquid, or solid form that are capable of producing incapacitation, injury, or death to exposed personnel. Other types of chemical agents, such as screening and signaling smokes, incendiaries, and flame agents, are not discussed in this manual; they are covered in FM 3–50, FM 20–33, FM 21–11, FM 21–40, and FM 23–30.

31. How Chemical Agents Can Enter Your Body

Chemical agents can enter your body through your eyes, nose, mouth, and skin. They can enter your body if agent vapors or liquid droplets get into your eyes. They can enter your body if you breathe contaminated air, if you eat contaminated food, or if you drink contaminated liquids. They can enter your body rapidly by absorption through breaks in the skin and more slowly through unbroken skin.

32. Characteristics of Chemical Agents

a. To master the proper protective measures to protect yourself against a chemical attack, you need to know the effects on your body of those chemical agents that may be used against you, your means of protection against these agents, and the decontamination and first-aid measures you must take if you become contaminated. Only this information is included in this chapter; however, if you are interested in learning more about chemical agents, consult TM 3–215.

b. You must protect yourself against chemical agents that may be used in any form to prevent you from accomplishing your mission. Agents may be disseminated in *liquid, solid, or gaseous* form; the liquid and solid forms may *vaporize*, causing a vapor hazard. For example, you may be hit with *liquid* blister agent from artillery fire; with tear agent which has been spread in *solid* form along a road or path; or with nerve agent in *gaseous* form. You must take protective action to prevent inhalation and skin absorption. Agents used in chemical operations will continue to be effective on your body, your clothing, and your equipment until they are removed or neutralized. Avoid any suspicious liquid or solid because it may be a chemical agent that could cause you to become a casualty. You must be alert.

33. Types of Agents

a. Agents Employed To Injure or Kill You. Certain agents may be used against you to cause injury or death—unless you are protected. If you are exposed and do not help yourself or receive immediate help, you will become a casualty and may die. Agents of this type are sometimes called casualty or casualty-producing agents. The chemical agents that may be employed to injure or kill you are—

(1) Nerve agents.

(2) Blister agents.

(3) Blood agents.

(4) Choking agents.

Of these, the two that you will be most likely to encouter are nerve agents and blister agents.

b. Agents Employed To Make You Temporarily Noneffective. Other agents may be used to make you temporarily noneffective for varying periods of time; however, you will fully recover from their effects. These agents are called incapacitating agents.

c. Agents Employed To Control Riots and To Train You. Still other agents that normally are used for riot control and for training may be used against you. These agents are used in protective mask training exercises, and you will completely recover from their effects in a short time without treatment. These are vomiting and tear agents. You may hear vomiting agent called Adamsite or DM and tear agents called CN and CS. The tear agent CS can be effectively employed in military operations against unprotected personnel if attacking troops quickly take advantage of its effects.

34. Nerve Agent Effects

a. Importance. Nerve agents are the most dangerous chemical agents because they very quickly cause casualties. The two types of nerve agents are G-agents and V-agents.

b. G-agents. G-agents normally will be disseminated in vapor form to cause casualties by inhalation. They also can be disseminated in liquid form to cause casualties by absorption through the skin and by ingestion of contaminated food or water. G-agents interfere with breathing and cause convulsions, paralysis, and death. When they are inhaled, their first effects on your body are unexplained runny nose, tightness in the chest, pinpointing of the eye pupils, and difficulty in breathing. You will not notice your own pupils pinpointing, but you may notice dimness of vision. When liquid agent is absorbed through the skin, there might be sweating and twitching in the area of the contamination, but the effects normally will parallel those for exposure to vapor form. These effects may not always occur or be noticed in the order given (particularly when the agent enters your body through the skin). However, they are vital warnings and must not be ignored. Without immediate decontamination and first aid, the early effects are usually followed by further difficulty in breathing, dizziness, headache, drooling, excessive sweating, stomach cramps, and involuntary urination and defecation.

c. V-agents. V-agents normally will be disseminated as liquid droplets to cause casualties by absorption through the skin. They also can be disseminated in vapor form to cause casualties by inhalation and by absorption through the skin. In either liquid or vapor form, V-agents affect the body in the same way it is affected by G-agents, and immediate decontamination and first-aid measures are necessary.

d. Actions You Should Take Immediately. Usually your first warning of exposure to a nerve agent is the effects it has on your body or on those around you. If you notice any of the effects described in *b* above, you must immediately stop breathing and mask and follow the decontamination and first-aid procedures outlined in paragraph 49.

35. Blister Agent Effects

a. Importance. Blister agents are important because they cause disabling burns in either vapor or liquid form. The blister agents include the mustards, arsenicals, and phosgene oxime. These agents penetrate the skin very rapidly; therefore, you must protect yourself quickly to avoid injury.

b. Effects. Blister agents damage any exposed skin surface. Light vapor concentrations cause damage that resembles severe sunburn, and liquids and heavy vapor concentrations cause blisters. Usually, the eyes and moist areas of the body are most affected. Blister agents have greater effects on the body when the skin is warm and moist, either from physical exertion or from the weather. The respiratory tract can be damaged by vapors, resulting in infections which could cause death. The digestive tract can be damaged by the consumption of food or water contaminated with blister agents. In vapor form, the arsenicals and phosgene oxime cause immediate eye pain, and in liquid form cause a strong stinging sensation of the skin. For the most part, the mustards do not cause immediate pain, and the effects may not be noticed for some time after exposure; however, the damage was done during the first few minutes after exposure even though you did not realize it. The extent of the damage will depend upon the concentration of the agent and the length of time you were exposed.

c. Actions You Should Take Immediately. At the first indication of a chemical attack, you must immediately stop breathing and mask, and, if contaminated, take the measures outlined in paragraph 50.

36. Blood Agent Effects

Blood agents cause casualties by inhalation. They act rapidly to prevent the blood from transferring oxygen to body tissue, and the lack of oxygen may cause suffocation and death. Difficult and *slow or rapid* breathing normally is the first effect. Without first aid, convulsions occur and death may follow when a large amount of the agent is inhaled. Eye and nose irritation, headache, and dizziness occur when a small amount is inhaled. A speedy death may occur or recovery may take place in a few hours, depending on the extent of exposure. Don your mask as it will provide complete protection against blood agents. Take the first-aid measures in paragraph 51.

37. Choking Agent Effects

Choking agents cause casualties by inhalation. They damange the lungs, causing them to fill with fluids. This prevents oxygen from reaching the body and death may result. The more serious effects usually occur after a period of time during which there are no symptoms. Repeated small exposures over short periods of time will cause casualties. Your protective mask provides complete protection if donned before exposure. Follow the first-aid measures in paragraph 52.

38. Incapacitating Agent Effects

a. General. Incapacitating agents may be of several types and produce temporary mental or physical effects, or both, which may cause you to be unable to properly perform your mission for a period of time. Incapacitating agents do not cause permanent damage.

b. Effects. Incapacitating agents are normally disseminated in aerosol form, as smokes or fine powders. Some are disseminated in vapor form. The physical effects vary but may include increased heart rate, dry skin and mouth, blurred vision, and slowing of activity, resulting in temporary inability to act normally. The mental effects vary but may include confusion, depression, and slowing of mental activity, resulting in temporary inability to think clearly and rationally. The protective mask provides protection against incapacitating agents if donned before exposure. Follow the decontamination and first-aid measures in paragraph 53.

39. Riot Control Agent Effects

a. General. Riot control agents cause temporary irritating effects. Vomiting and tear agents are the two types of such agents. They may be used in conjunction with other agents to decrease your fighting efficiency and to lower your ability to protect yourself against other chemical agents. The protective mask will provide complete protection against these agents if donned before exposure.

b. Vomiting Agents. The effects of vomiting agents are vomiting, coughing, sneezing, pain in the nose and throat, nasal discharge, and tears. Headache often follows. As the effects may be delayed several minutes, there is a possibility that you may inhale enough vomiting agent to make you sick before you realize the agent is present and mask. Adamsite (DM) is a vomiting agent. Follow first-aid measures in paragraph 54*a*.

c. Tear Agents. Tear agents produce sharp, irritating pain in the eyes, resulting in an abundant flow of tears; the effects wear off quickly. For a short time you may not be able to see. CN, CN solution, and CS are tear agents. The effects of CS on the eyes are more intense than the effects of CN; and, in addition, CS causes sneezing and runny nose, coughing, chest tightness, difficult breathing, and stinging of moist skin. In high concentrations it may cause nausea and vomiting. CN and CS are used in training exercises to test the fit and operation of your protective mask and to prove to you that it provides complete protection against inhalation of harmful chemical agents. Follow decontamination and first-aid measures in paragraph 54b.

40. Protection Against Chemical Agents

Now that you know the effects of chemical agents you realize that unless you are alert and protect yourself, you may become a casualty as a result of chemical operations. Items that will be available to aid you in protection against chemical agents are described below. You must become completely familiar with them and must be able to use them correctly and automatically.

a. *Your Protective Mask.* Your protective mask is your best protection against chemical agents in vapor or aerosol form. In fact, it is so important to you that much of this manual deals with it separately. Complete references on your mask are given in paragraph 11. Whenever you want to find something concerning it or need to refresh yourself on any point, refer to paragraph 11 to find the exact place to look for the information you need. You must know *how* to don and care for your mask and *when* to mask without order or alarm. You must be able to accomplish the following actions in 9 seconds or less:

(1) Stop breathing.

(2) Remove headgear (and eyeglasses, if worn).

(3) Mask.

(4) Clear mask by blocking outlet and exhaling.

(5) Check mask for leaks by closing inlet valve assemblies and inhaling.

b. *Protective Clothing and Covering.*

(1) The protection afforded by the field uniform can be greatly increased by a treatment called impregnating. Impregnated (permeable protective) clothing will protect you against vapors and small droplets of blister agents and V-agents for a limited period of time; drops larger than 3 millimeters (1/8 inch) in diameter will go through impregnated clothing quickly. You may be issued the chemical protective liner outfit. This uniform is worn under the seasonal outergarment and will give you the same protection as the present two-layer impregated uniform.

(2) Any kind of covering available will help protect you against a surprise spray attack. Quickly cover yourself with your poncho or shelter half because spray reaches the ground in only a few seconds.

Cover as much of your body as possible, particularly your head and neck. Gloves that give hand and wrist protection should be worn. After the spray has stopped falling, throw off the protective cover, taking care to keep the liquid off your skin and clothing.

c. M5A4 Protection and Treatment Set or the M13 Individual Decontaminating and Reimpregnating Kit. The M5A4 protection and treatment set or the M13 individual decontaminating and reimpregnating kit will be issued you as an accessory to the field protective mask.

(1) M5 protective ointment will protect exposed skin surfaces if applied before exposure to blister agents and V-agents. It may be used for decontamination of liquid agent on the skin and also for emergency decontamination of your clothing and individual equipment.

(*a*) After masking, rub a thin coating of protective ointment on the skin around the edges of the mask, on the neck, and on the hands to protect exposed skin at the first indication of a chemical attack or when a chemical attack is expected. M5 protective ointment may also be used immediately after exposure for decontaminating blister agents and V-agents. It is harmful to the eyes; it should never be put in the eyes or on the skin around the eyes. Do not allow it to enter your mouth. Use the following procedures for decontaminating liquid agent on the skin (fig. 7) :

1. *Pinch blot* the liquid from the skin with a cloth from your protection and treatment set.

2. Flush the area with water.

3. Apply and rub in protective ointment. Keep it away from your eyes and mouth.

4. Remove ointment from the skin with another cloth.

5. Reapply ointment and let it stay on.

(b) In an emergency, decontaminate your clothing and individual equipment with M5 protective ointment. Blot the liquid agent, flush with water, rub on protective ointment, remove it, reapply, and allow it to remain. Use this procedure for parts of your equipment that you will touch. Use this procedure to decontaminate your mask, but remove all excess ointment after the last application to prevent it from getting into your eyes and mouth.

(2) The M13 individual decontaminating and reimpregnating kit contains material for decontaminating your skin, individual equipment, and clothing and for emergency reimpregnation of the protective liner outfit.

(a) Any chemical agent that has not penetrated the skin may be decontaminated

ACT FAST!

PINCH BLOT AGENT

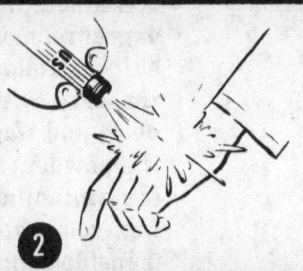

FLUSH

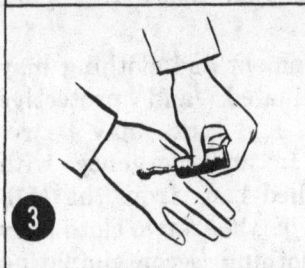

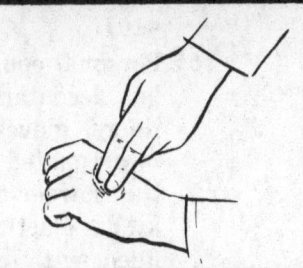

APPLY OINTMENT AND RUB IN

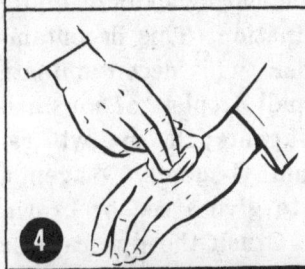

REMOVE OINTMENT

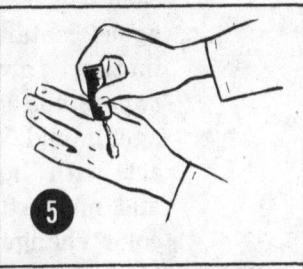

REAPPLY OINTMENT AND LET IT STAY ON

Figure 7. How to remove liquid agent from your skin with M5 protective ointment.

with the skin decontaminating powder, contained in a pad. Immediately after exposure, mask, and decontaminate the skin as follows: *Blot* any liquid from the skin with the pad; *turn* the pad over, and *slap* it on the skin to release the powder; then *rub* the powder over the contaminated area. If after masking, you suspect that a chemical agent is inside your mask, use the skin decontaminating pad in the same manner to decontaminate your mask (see para 41*b*).

(*b*) Personal equipment and clothing may be decontaminated, and protective liners, gloves, and socks may be re-impregnated in an emergency with the powder-filled bags from the M13 kit. A plastic bag holds two cloth bags filled with clothing decontaminating powder; a dye capsule is included in each bag for indicating spots of liquid agent contamination. This decontaminating powder will decontaminate vapors and small droplets of mustard agents and V-agents; the dye will react with liquid G-agents, V-agents, and mustard to give a red or brown color change. Crush the dye capsule by working it into a corner of the bag and grinding it between the palms of the hands. Mix the dye with the powder by kneading the bag for a *full minute.* The cloth bag may be used for decontaminating up to 24 hours after the dye is mixed with the powder. Use one bag for clothing and the other for equipment decontamination.

1. Decontamination (wear protective mask and gloves). Dust and lightly rub the outer garments, beginning with the gloves. Inspect any wet spots *before* and during dusting, and rub them to detect the brown or red color change if they are liquid agents. Cut away colored spots from clothing with the cutter included in the M13 kit. Dust any exposed underwear. Dust and rub equipment (rifle, pack) with the second bag. Metal objects, particularly weapons, must be carefully cleaned and oiled after decontamination; remove all powder by any means available, and oil. Completely field strip and clean weapons at the earliest opportunity.

2. Reimpregnation. The two cloth bags may be used for emergency reimpregnation of the chemical protective liner outfit, consisting of trouser and shirt liners, socks, and gloves. The bags *cannot* be used for this purpose after being used for decontamination. Two methods of reimpregnation are described below.

(a) *Ground method* (wear protective mask and gloves during reimpregnation). Spread out trouser liner on poncho (if poncho is not available, spread trouser liner on uncontaminated ground). Using one large bag (do not crush capsule), pat a small section (1 foot by 1 foot, approximately) of the outer surface of the trouser liner with bag to deposit the powder on the liner. Rub the powder into the fabric. Repeat this procedure until the outside of the trouser liner is completely covered. If powder is still left in the bag, reduce those parts which are not as white as other parts. Make sure that the crotch of the trouser liner is well dusted. Save a small amount of the powder in the bag and dust the socks in the manner described above. Place the shirt liner on the poncho (or ground) and, using the other large bag, treat in the same way as the trouser liner. Make sure that the armpits of the shirt liner are well dusted. Use the last small amount of powder for treating gloves. To treat gloves, dust and rub the powder into them while they are being worn.

(b) *Nonremoval method* (reimpregnation while wearing liner). Remove outer clothing (down to the protective liner). Continue wearing the protective mask and gloves. Using the buddy system, each buddy should treat the other's protective liner by use of the same patting and rubbing procedure described in (a) above. To avoid excessive loss of powder when using this method, do not pat as hard with the bag as when reimpregnating clothing on the ground.

d. Vesicant Gas Resistant Leather Dressing. This dressing, when properly applied, makes leather resistant to penetration by chemical agents. The hot-dip method is the most effective method for applying the dressing to combat leather boots. This normally is done by your unit. The procedure for the hot-dip method is outlined in FM 21-40. After boots have been worn for an extended period of time or have been washed, wet, or decontaminated, it may be necessary to replenish leather dressing to insure maximum protection. The hot-dip method should be used if the materials are available and the situation permits. As an emergency measure, the dressing may be applied by hand; you will be issued the leather dressing to treat your boots. Apply the dressing to the inside and outside surfaces of clean boots; be sure to cover all seams.

41. Decontamination and First Aid

a. *General.* Decontamination is the act of removing, neutralizing, or destroying contamination. First aid is the emergency care (help) that you can give yourself or your buddy before trained medical help can be reached. If you cannot prevent contamination by taking protective actions, then you must quickly decontaminate your body. Decontamination does not repair injury to the body; it only prevents further damage from being caused. Therefore, if you notice any agent effects after decontaminating, you must immediately take proper first-aid measures.

b. *Decontamination of Eyes, Face, and Mask.* Immediate decontamination of agent in the eyes, on the face, and inside the mask is necessary to prevent your becoming a casualty. If you believe you have agent in your eyes or on your face, after masking, seek overhead cover to protect you while you carry out the decontamination procedure outlined below. If no overhead cover is available, use your poncho for protection against further liquid contamination. If possible, use the buddy system to lessen the time required for decontamination.

(1) Remove and open your canteen.
(2) Prepare the skin decontaminating pad from your M13 kit (or M5 ointment) for use.
(3) Hold your breath.
(4) Remove your mask.
(5) Flush your eyes with water.
(6) Using the skin decontaminating pad or M5 ointment, decontaminate your face

and the portion of your mask that came in contact with the contamination on your face (para 40c).

Caution. Be careful to keep M5 ointment or powder from the skin, decontaminating pad out of your eyes and mouth; remove excess from your face and mask after decontamination.

(7) Replace mask and resume breathing.

The decontamination procedure should be repeated until you are sure that all contamination has been removed from your eyes, face, and the inside of your mask.

c. First Aid. First aid is a necessary skill. If you cannot decontaminate a chemical agent before it is absorbed through your eyes or skin or if you inhale it, you must be able to take the proper first-aid measures to keep from becoming a casualty. Anything you can do to keep yourself or your buddy in fighting condition is your responsibility. Watch for any clues that will tell you that you have been exposed to a chemical agent. You may see the agent, smell it, sense its presence, or you may hear something to tell you that a chemical attack has occurred. Watch for any body changes in yourself or your buddy that indicate you have been exposed to a chemical agent. Chemical agents act fast; therefore, you must act faster. Do as much as you can, within the limits of your mission, to help yourself and your buddy. First-aid measures you must take for different types of chemical agents are given in paragraphs 46 through 61. You must take these measures quickly to avoid becoming a casualty.

42. When to Remove Your Mask

a. You must always remember to wear your mask after a chemical attack until told it is safe to remove it. You must not remove your mask until tests prove that the area is free of chemical agents.

THE DECISION TO UNMASK IS ALWAYS MADE BY THE PERSON IN COMMAND.

b. After a chemical attack, the person in command will have tests made with a chemical agent detector kit to determine if the area is free of agent. He will follow the procedures outlined in FM 21–40.

c. A small detached group, or a group that has become isolated, may not have a chemical agent detector kit to make tests for the presence of a chemical agent. If your mission permits and you are the ranking member of such a group, you must make every effort to lead the group back to your unit or to another unit where a detector kit is available. You and your buddies must continue to wear your masks. If the mission does not permit the group to join a unit, the field expedient action outlined below may be taken after you have worn your masks for an extended period of time.

    (1) Have two or three men each take a deep breath, hold it, and break the seals of their masks, keeping your eyes wide open for about 15 seconds. Have the men rees-

tablish the mask seals, and observe them in a shaded area for 10 minutes for symptoms of exposure to any chemical agent, particularly nerve agent.

(2) If no symptoms develop, have these same men break the seals of their masks and take three or four breaths. Have the men reestablish the mask seals, and again observe them in a shaded area for 10 minutes for symptoms of exposure to any chemical agent.

(3) If no symptoms develop, have these men unmask for 5 minutes. Have the men remask, and after 10 minutes, examine them in a shaded area for symptoms of exposure to any chemical agent.

(4) If no symptoms develop, have the entire group remove their masks. All personnel should remain alert for symptoms of exposure to any chemical agent.

This procedure requires such limited exposure that no serious ill effects will be suffered from any chemical agent that may be present. If symptoms of nerve agent exposure occur, decontaminate as appropriate and administer one injection of atropine; if symptoms of exposure to other agents occur, apply decontamination and first-aid measures.

d. If you are isolated as an individual, continue to wear your mask and make every effort to find your way to your unit or to another unit. If this is not possible, wear your mask for an extended period of time, then follow the procedure outlined in *c* above. Since you cannot detect pinpointing of your eye pupils, always remain alert for symptoms of exposure to any chemical agent.

e. Before using the unmasking procedure described in *c* above, you should observe the area for signs of any chemical agent (para 44). Observe the ground and vegetation for chemical agents in solid or liquid form; look for smokes and mists; look for signs of munitions used for disseminating chemical agents. Observe the animals, insects, and birds in the area, since they are also affected by chemical agents. Be sure you know the effects of chemical agents on yourself and others; and, if symptoms occur, immediately stop breathing, don your mask, and take necessary decontamination and first-aid measures.

Section II. THINGS TO DO DURING A CHEMICAL ATTACK

43. Continue Your Mission

Stay alert and be ready to take the protective actions you have learned without order or alarm. Remember that taking the proper protective actions will enable you to continue your mission and remain an effective fighting man.

44. Chemical Agent Detection

Your unit will have detection devices that will be used by specially trained personnel to detect and identify chemical agents (para 46). However, your five physical senses are valuable aids in detecting chemical agents that may be harmful to you. You must train your senses to aid you in detecting chemical agents. Detection devices should always be used to determine whether your suspicions are correct because there are limitations and shortcomnigs in detecting chemcial agents by your senses. Detection by the five physical senses is discussed below.

a. Your Sense of Feeling. A feeling of irritation in the eyes, nose, or throat or on the skin is an urgent warning to protect yourself. This, along with other effects as headache, dizziness, and nausea, occurs upon exposure to several of the chemical agents. These general effects cannot be used to determine what chemical agent is present, but rather, they will serve as a warning that some agent probably is present. You should immediately stop breathing and mask and take necessary decontamination and first-aid measures.

b. Your Sense of Smell. You will learn rapidly to identify those odors which are common to the battlefield. Anything which smells strange, unfamiliar, or out of the ordinary must be suspected of being a chemical agent. Most chemical agents have very faint odors or none at all. Also, the agents with detectable odors often smell different to different individuals. Some agents can be present in amounts sufficient to produce harmful effects without giving off detectable odors. Also, continued exposure to a chemical agent may dull your sense of smell to the point where harmful concentrations can be present before an odor is evident. The enemy may mix harmful chemical agents or change characteristic odors to confuse you. Detection of chemical agents by smell is by no means a reliable method; but if you smell anything strange, unfamiliar, or out of the ordinary, immediately stop breathing and mask.

c. Your Sense of Sight. You must be alert for the possible means of dissemination of chemical agents and for their effects an you and on your buddies.

(1) Since chemical agents may be in one of three forms—solid, liquid, or vapor—your sense of sight may help you detect their presence. Mustard, unless of a purified type, is dark brown in its liquid state. As a liquid it may be easy to detect and would appear as dark oily patches on leaves and buildings. However, mustard changes slowly to a colorless vapor. Nerve agents may be either colorless liquids or colorless vapors. Although you cannot see blister agents or nerve agents in their gaseous states, you may be able to see the munitions the enemy uses to spread them. Most chemical agents have some color in the liquid or solid states, and some can be seen in the vapor state as mist or thin fog immediately after bombs or shells burst. Chemical agents may appear to be smoke or may be hid-

den in smoke clouds. Know the conditions for masking (para 45).

(2) Since your first indication of a chemical attack may be the effects of a chemical agent, be alert for signs of the effects in yourself and in those around you. Be sure you know the effects and the proper protective actions and decontamination and first-aid measures to take.

d. Your Sense of Hearing. Any seeming differences in explosive sounds of shell or bomb bursts cannot be taken as indications of a chemical attack, but suspicious sounds should make you look for other indications of such attacks. If you hear anything strange or unusual, even though you cannot see what has happened, mask until you suspicions are checked out.

e. Your Sense of Taste. A strange flavor in food, water, or cigarettes may mean that they are contaminated. Do not put anything into your mouth that you suspect of being contaminated.

45. Conditions for Masking Without Order or Alarm

Automatic masking is necessary once chemical operations have been initiated or information is available that they are about to be initiated. You will mask without order or alarm every time any one of the conditions shown in figure 8 occurs, and you must wear your mask until told to unmask. Study figure 8; remember the conditions for masking and what to do when an attack is suspected (fig. 8).

WHEN TO MASK

Once chemical or biological agents have been used, are suspected of having been used, or information is available that they are about to be used,

MASK WITHOUT ORDER OR ALARM WHEN····

1 YOUR POSITION IS HIT BY
    artillery or mortar fire
    missiles or rockets
    smoke or mists
    aerial spray or bombs

2 SMOKE FROM AN UNKOWN SOURCE IS PRESENT

3 A SUSPICIOUS ODOR, LIQUID, OR SOLID IS PRESENT

4 YOU ARE ENTERING AN AREA SUSPECTED OF BEING
    CONTAMINATED

5 YOU HAVE ONE OR MORE OF THE FOLLOWING
    SYMPTOMS

    an unexplained runny nose

    a feeling of choking or tightness in the chest
      or throat

    dimming of vision

    irritation of the eyes

    difficulty in or increased rate of breathing

*Figure 8. How to protect yourself under chemical
or biological attack.*

WHAT TO DO

UNDER KNOWN OR SUSPECTED CHEMICAL OR BIOLOGICAL ATTACK---

1. STOP BREATHING.

2. MASK.

3. GIVE ALARM.

4. CONTINUE YOUR MISSION.

5. REMAIN MASKED UNTIL ORDERED TO UNMASK.

IF...

the situation permits--
TAKE OVERHEAD COVER.

your eyes or skin is contaminated--
DECONTAMINATE.

you have symptoms of nerve agent poisoning--
TAKE ATROPINE.

your clothing and equipment are contaminated--
DECONTAMINATE WHEN THE MISSION PERMITS.

Figure 8—Continued.

Section III. THINGS TO DO AFTER
A CHEMICAL ATTACK

46. Chemical Agent Detection and Identification

After a chemical agent attack, the agent must be identified to assist you in properly protecting and decontaminating yourself. During an attack, you might suspect the identity of the agent; however, this suspicion should be confirmed. Your unit will have chemical agent detector kits that will detect and identify chemical agents in both vapor and liquid forms.

47. Actions to Take When in Contaminated Areas

Avoid contaminated areas or pass through these areas as rapidly as possible, if your mission permits. If you must remain in or pass through contaminated areas, you should:

a. Use all the protective equipment you have to prevent chemical agents from entering your body.

b. When possible, use vehicles and travel upwind of the contaminated area.

c. Select routes or bivouac areas on high ground since chemical agents tend to be heavier than air and settle in low places. Avoid cellars, trenches, gullies, valleys, and other low places where agents may collect.

d. Avoid unnecessary contact with contaminated surfaces (such as buildings, debris, woods, shrubbery, tall grass, and puddles) which tend to hold the agent.

e. Do not stir up dust unnecessarily.

48. Protect Your Feet

When a chemical agent is present in liquid or solid form, you are almost certain to get some on your boots from the contaminated ground and vegetation. Liquid nerve and blister agents penetrate leather boots very rapidly if they are not treated with leather dressing. Care for your boots as described in paragraph 40*d*.

49. Decontamination and First Aid for Nerve Agents

a. If you believe you have agent in your eyes, on your face, or inside your mask follow the instructions in paragraph 41*b*. You will not know what the agent is, so don't waste time trying to decide. Then, immediately remove agent from any other exposed skin as described in paragraph 40*c*(1)(*a*) or (2)(*a*). Continue your mission.

b. Use atropine for counteracting the effects of nerve agent and give artificial respiration for improving or restoring breathing.

    (1) *When to use atropine.* If you notice any of the early effects of nerve agent poisoning in yourself or in those around you, mask, and give an injection of atropine at once. If a buddy is unable to help himself, quickly remove any agent from his eyes and face, check his mask or put it on him, then give him an injection of atropine, using his atropine injector if possible. The early effects are listed below but they will not necessarily occur, or may not be noticed, in this order.

    (*a*) Unexplained runny nose.

(b) Tightness in the chest or difficulty in breathing.

(c) Blurring or dimming of vision.

(d) Shrinking of the pupils of your buddy's eyes to pinpoint size. Since you will not notice your own pupils pinpointing, a buddy may tell you. Difficulty in seeing or in focusing your eyes is also an indication that the pupils have pinpointed.

(2) *How to use the automatic atropine injector.*

(a) You must know the procedure outlined in (b) below for using the automatic atropine injector. If you need atropine, you will not have time to read these instructions. The injector and directions for its use are illustrated in figure 9.

(b) The spring-operated automatic atropine injector contains 2 milligrams of atropine, and is designed for ease of operation. The injector is a white plastic tube, with a blue cap on the functioning end and a red safety cap on the other end. The red safety cap is serrated for touch identification in darkness. (Atropine injectors procured in the future will be green with a green cap on the functioning end and a yellow safety cap. There will be a period of time when there are injec-

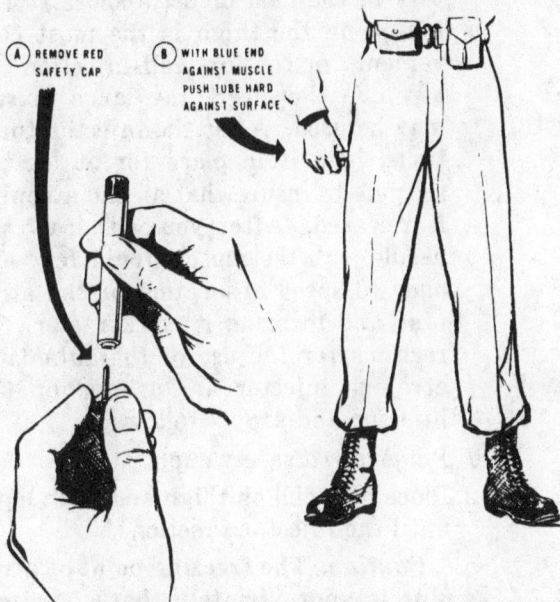

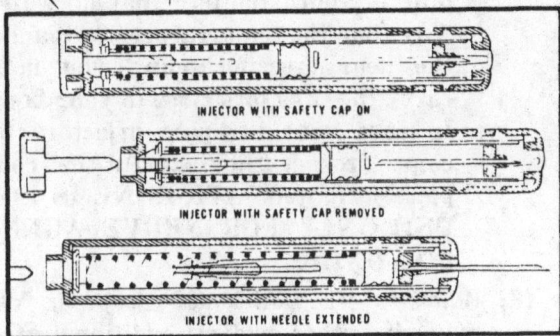

A—Remove the red safety cap
B—With blue end against muscle, push tube hard against surface
Diagram of atropine automatic injector

Figure 9. How to use the automatic atropine injector.

tors in the field of both colors.) The muscle in the thigh is the most convenient place for self-injection of atropine; however, any large muscle may be used. After the injector functions, hold it in place for at least 3 seconds to insure that all the atropine is released. After you withdraw the needle, rub the muscle for a few seconds to speed absorption of the atropine and to make it work faster. Directions for the use of the automatic atropine injector are printed on the injector and are as follows:

1. Remove *red* safety cap.
2. Place *blue* end on thigh and push hard until the injector functions.

Caution. **The freezing point of atropine is approximately that of water. Any time the temperature approaches the near freezing point, you must carry the injectors close to your body. In case your atropine injectors become frozen, they should be completely thawed. ATROPINE IS FOR USE ONLY FOR NERVE AGENT POISONING.**

(3) *When to give additional atropine.* You may give other soldiers additional atropine if the early effects continue or reappear or if additional effects are noted. Excessive perspiring, drooling, difficulty in breathing, nausea or vomiting, jerk-

ing and twitching of muscles, and involuntary urination or defecation are symptoms that indicate the need for additional atropine. You are issued three automatic atropine injectors. You may give as many as three injections of atropine at 10-minute intervals if symptoms do not begin to disappear. The need for additional atropine injections should be determined by a medical officer or aidman. If neither is present, the need may be determined by an officer or noncommissioned officer. The highest ranking person present will tell you when to give more than three injections.

(4) *When to give artificial respiration.* If a soldier's breathing becomes weak or stops, he must be given artificial respiration in addition to atropine. He must be masked before artificial respiration is begun in a contaminated area. If he is already masked, quickly remove the mask, wipe away any fluids that may have collected in his mouth or in his mask, and replace the mask. Observe him closely while giving artificial respiration to insure that his breathing passageway remains clear. Continue artificial respiration until normal breathing is resumed. If another person is helping you, one can give the atropine injection while the other is attending to the mask and giving artificial respira-

tion. Do not delay artificial respiration to loosen clothing, to warm the casualty, or to give stimulants. The preferred method of artificial respiration is the mouth-to-mouth method; however, it cannot be used in a contaminated area. The chest-pressure arm-lift method (modified Silvester method) should be used in a contaminated area. These methods are described in FM 21-11.

c. If the early effects of nerve agent poisoning were present and you took one injection of atropine, you do not require rest, evacuation, or further treatment unless the effects persist or additional effects develop. After you have taken atropine, continue your mission. Help others who cannot help themselves if the situation permits.

d. Observe the following precautions when you have reason to believe you have been exposed to a nerve agent.

(1) Do not inject atropine until you are sure it is needed. Unexplained runny nose, tightness in your chest and difficulty in breathing, blurring or dimming of vision, and pinpointing of the eye pupils are signs that you need atropine.

(2) Do not neglect your mission. If you give yourself atropine as soon as you notice the early effects of a nerve agent, you will have a better chance to continue your duties without delay. Dryness of the mouth and freer breathing are signs

that you are getting relief and have had enough atropine to overcome the effects of the nerve agent.

(3) Watch for continued or additional effects (*b*(3) above) of nerve agent poisoning in yourself or a buddy that will require additional atropine injections.

(4) Avoid water and food that may be contaminated with nerve agent. If you have swallowed food or water which may be contaminated and any of these effects occur—increased flow of saliva, nausea, pains in the stomach, or tightness in the chest—take atropine.

50. Decontamination and First Aid for Blister Agents

a. Immediately following the first indication of a chemical attack, particularly a blister agent attack, apply M5 protective ointment, if issued, as described in paragraph 40*c*(1)(*a*) after masking. If you believe you have agent in your eyes or on your face, follow the instructions in paragraph 41*b*. You will not know what the agent is, so don't waste time trying to decide. Then, immediately remove agent from any other exposed skin as described in paragraph 40*c*(1)(*a*) or (2)(*a*).

b. If blisters form, avoid breaking them; if blisters break, treat the areas as open wounds to prevent infection. Blister agent may burn away some of the skin; treat these areas as heat burns. The damage to the skin is the same as the damage from a heat burn. Apply the first-aid measures outlined in FM 21–11.

51. First Aid for Blood Agents

The first-aid measures for blood agent poisoning are inhalation of amyl nitrite and artificial respiration. If you are issued amyl nitrite, use it yourself or help a buddy use it. Squeeze an ampul until it pops, and insert it inside the facepiece of your mask under the eyepiece. Repeat this at intervals of 3 or 4 minutes until normal breathing returns or until a total of eight ampuls have been used. If you are not issued amyl nitrite, an aidman will give it to you.

52. First Aid for Choking Agents

Loosen clothing. Even if you have inhaled some choking agent, continue your duties. If undue shortness of breath, chest tightness, or painful coughs occur, keep warm, take it easy, and avoid unnecessary movement.

53. Decontamination and First Aid for Incapacitating Agents

When a buddy is exposed to an incapacitating agent, move him into fresh air, if possible, and observe him closely. Flush the eyes with plain water only. *Your* main safeguard is to recognize the symptoms in yourself and request help from your buddy or report to medical personnel as soon as possible.

54. First Aid for Riot Control Agents

a. Vomiting Agents. Wear your mask in spite of coughing, sneezing, drooling, or nausea. Take a breath, hold it, and lift the mask from the face briefly, if necessary to vomit or drain saliva from the facepiece. Clear your mask each time you lift it from your face and before you resume breathing. Continue your mission as soon as you have masked; vigorous activity helps reduce the nausea and shortens its duration.

b. Tear Agents. Keep your eyes open as much as possible. When vision clears, continue your mission. When you are told it is safe to remove your mask, face into the wind, keeping your eyes open. Blot away tears, but do not rub your eyes. If agent gets into your eyes, follow the instructions in paragraph 41*b*.

55. Decontamination

Decontamination of a chemical agent is the act of removing, neutralizing, or destroying the agent. The following paragraphs will serve as guidelines in methods of decontamination.

56. Decontamination of Your Body

a. General. If you are subjected to a chemical attack, you must decontaminate the exposed surfaces of your body as quickly as possible to avoid serious injury or death. You will not know what agent has been used, so don't waste time trying to decide. If decontamination is not accomplished quickly and completely, first-aid measures are necessary. The items available to you for decontamination of your body are water, soap, and either M5 protective ointment or the skin decontaminating pad from the M13 kit.

b. Your Eyes and Face. Chemical agents are more rapidly absorbed through the eyes than through other skin surfaces of the body. You must decontaminate immediately if you believe that you have agent in your eyes or on your face. Follow the instructions in paragraph 41b.

c. *Your Skin.* Speed is essential in removing liquid agent from the skin. If the agent penetrates the skin, it cannot be removed or neutralized. Follow the instructions in paragraph 40c-(1) (a) or (2) (a).

57. Decontamination of Clothing and Footwear

a. *Clothing.* If the situation permits, items of clothing that are contaminated should be removed and decontaminated. Airing for 24 hours in moderate temperature normally will rid clothing of vapor contamination. If clothing is contaminated with liquid agent, it should be washed in hot soapy water. When the situation does not permit you to remove contaminated clothing, use M5 ointment or the clothing decontaminating bag from the M13 kit to decontaminate small areas; follow instructions in paragraph 40c(1)(b) or (2)(b).

b. *Footwear.* Decontaminate footwear by scrubbing with a stiff brush, using hot soapy water; rinse, air, and apply leather dressing (para 40d).

58. Decontamination of Individual Equipment

The method and items that you use to decontaminate your equipment will depend on their availability and the time in which you have to accomplish decontamination. Those portions of the equipment that you will come in direct contact with need decontamination first. Soap and water, gasoline, kerosene, and heat are effective decontaminants; weathering is also effective. If issued, use M5 protective ointment to decontaminate items of individual equipment (para 40c(1)(b)); or use your clothing decontaminating bag from the M13 kit for individual equipment except your mask (para 40c(2)(b)). If you have the M13 kit, use the skin decontaminating pad to decontaminate your mask (para 40c(2)(a)). Do not use boiling water to decontaminate your mask as it may damage the eyelenses; water will damage the filter elements of the mask.

59. Decontamination of Food and Water

a. Food. If your rations are open and become exposed to contamination, bury them. Wash canned food containers with hot soapy water before opening.

b. Water. Drink water from approved sources only. Do not attempt to decontaminate water that is contaminated by chemical agents.

60. Reporting

It is your responsibility to report any information that you are aware of pertaining to a chemical attack. This report should be made immediately to your leader.

61. Marking of Contaminated Areas

After a chemical attack, the contaminated area should be marked (para 10d). The standard chemical contamination marker is shown in figure 2. The triangular marker is yellow on both sides, and the word GAS in red is on the side facing away from the contamination. The name of the agent (if known) and the date and time of detection will be placed on the back of the marker. Study this marker and remember it. Do not enter areas that are posted with this marker unless you are ordered to do so. You may encounter contaminated areas that have not been marked; therefore, you must always remain alert for indications of chemical agent contamination.

CHAPTER 3

PROCEDURES IN BIOLOGICAL OPERATIONS

Section I. THINGS TO DO BEFORE
A BIOLOGICAL ATTACK

62. General

This chapter explains how biological agents may be used against you and describes the individual actions that you must take to minimize the possibility of your becoming a casualty. If these living agents are used, you must be able to protect yourself against them during and after an attack. You must know the characteristics of biological agents, how they may be used against you, and how they can enter your body. This chapter contains important information that will help you and your buddies protect yourselves and continue your mission if biological weapons are used against you.

63. How the Enemy Can Attack You

a. Biological agents can be disseminated as aerosols by generators, explosives, missiles, and manned or unmanned aircraft. A biological agent aerosol is composed of tiny particles which are smaller than dust particles. The aerosol may be released on or off the target area depending on the munition used. Air currents will spread the aerosol, and, if unmasked, you will inhale it.

b. Biological agents may be disseminated by the release of living insects (vectors), such as flies, mosquitoes, fleas, and ticks, on the target. Normally, the agent will be transmitted to you through their bites; however, agents can be transmitted to your food or water or to cuts and scratches on your skin by contaminated vectors.

64. Biological Agents Defined

Biological agents are microorganisms (germs) which cause disease in man, plants, or animals or cause deterioration of materiel. Only those biological agents that can be used to cause disease in man are covered in this manual. If you are interested in learning more about types of biological agents, consult TM 3–216.

65. How Biological Agents Can Enter Your Body

Biological agents can enter your body through your nose, mouth, and skin, depending on the method of agent release.

a. Biological agents in aerosol form normally will enter your body through your nose or mouth and will be taken into the lungs.

b. Biological agents can also enter your body through your mouth if you use contaminated food or water, and they will be taken into your digestive system. If your hands are contaminated, the germs may be spread to your mouth when you eat, drink, or smoke. Any contaminated object placed in your mouth can allow the germs to enter, and they will be taken into your digestive system. Germs can also enter the skin through cuts and scratches.

c. Biological agents delivered by living vectors can enter your body by the bites of the vectors or through your broken skin. The agent then enters the bloodstream, resulting in infection.

d. Remember that although biological agents can enter your body through contaminated food, water, and objects and by vector bites, the main danger in a biological agent attack is breathing the agent aerosols. Your protective mask, if properly fitted and worn, will prevent agents in aerosol form from entering your body by inhalation.

66. Characteristics of Biological Agents

a. Some microorganisms cause disease, some are used to produce material (serums or antitoxins) to prevent disease, and others are used to produce material (antibiotics—penicillin, stroptomycin, aureomycin) to fight disease. Still others are used by industries in making bread, beer, vinegar, and cheese; in manufacturing textiles; and in tanning leather. Only a relatively few types of microorganisms cause disease; even fewer are so infective and so hardy that they can be used as biological agents.

b. Normally, the particles in a biological agent aerosol cannot be seen as they travel downwind, and they go wherever air can go. The particles can be inhaled as you breathe and infection may occur that can result in sickness and death. Your protective mask will protect you from breathing the aerosol. The biological agent aerosol can contaminate food and water supplies, clothing, and equipment. Some of the biological agents may live in the target area, which may range in thousands of square kilometers, for long periods of time. However, microorganisms are living matter, and they behave as do other living things. They reproduce, breathe, eat, grow, and die. They depend on oxygen, moisture, food, and certain limits of temperature for life and growth. Most types of microorganisms die when their surroundings do not provide the required conditions for their survival. Therefore, exposure to sunlight or to unfavorable conditions will cause the majority of the microorganisms in a biological agent aerosol to die within a short time. Most microorganisms can be killed by such simple acts as boiling, cooking, or exposing to sunlight; and they can be removed from your skin and equipment with soap and water.

c. Biological agents disseminated by vectors, usually insects, can live in the bodies of the vectors for varying periods of time. Some vectors can pass the microorganisms on to their next generation.

d. Biological agents cannot be detected by your five physical senses.

e. Biological agents do not produce immediate effects on your body. The time between exposure to an agent and the beginning of disease symptoms (known as the incubation period) can vary from days to weeks, depending upon the agent used. Men exposed to equal amounts of an agent will react differently. Some may escape disease entirely, others may have very mild attacks, while still others may become seriously ill.

67. Protective Measures You Can Take Before A Biological Attack

a. *Maintain Natural Body Defenses.* A healthy body can better resist disease and infection from any source. Therefore, keep yourself in top physical shape, get as much rest as you can, and exercise your body. A high standard of personal cleanliness and careful attention to field sanitation also are good insurance against the spread of disease, regardless of its source. Keep your body, your clothes, and your living area clean. Care for minor wounds, cuts, and scratches by keeping them clean and using available first-aid supplies. Such care speeds healing and reduces the possibility of infection from any source. Soap and water are very effective in keeping cuts and scratches clean.

b. *Take All Prescribed Immunizations or Other Medication.* You already know that the Army has a varied and effective immunization program. In the event of biological weapons employment, you may be given additional immunizations or issued special medications. Immunizations are valuable because they strengthen the body's defense against certain diseases. If you are attacked with biological agents, your immunizations may prevent disease, or will reduce the severity of the disease.

c. *Train In the Use of Your Protective Mask.* You and your buddies must know how to use and care for your protective masks. In fact, your mask is so important to you that much of this manual deals with it separately. Complete references on your mask are given in paragraph 11.

Whenever you want to find something concerning it or need to refresh yourself on any point, refer to paragraph 11 to find the exact place to look for the information you need. You must know *how* to don and care for your mask and *when* to mask and to unmask. Learn the conditions for automatic masking without order or alarm (para 71).

68. Decontamination and First Aid

The simplest and most effective method to decontaminate your body after a biological agent attack is to use soap and water. Decontamination is discussed in paragraph 74. There are no first-aid measures you can take for biological agents because there are no immediate effects. Treatment of casualties is discussed in paragraph 75.

Section II. THINGS TO DO DURING A BIOLOGICAL ATTACK

69. Biological Agent Detection

Biological agents are hard to detect in the field. You cannot detect their presence with your physical senses; but there are certain clues that may warn you of or cause you to suspect a biological attack. You can assist in detection by reporting to your leaders any of the following suspicious items or circumstances:

a. Enemy aircraft dropping unidentified material or spraying unidentified substances.

b. New and unusual types of shells and bombs, particularly those which burst with little or no blast.

c. Smokes from an unknown source or of an unknown nature.

d. An increased occurrence of sick or dead animals.

e. Unusual or unexplained increase in the number of insects, such as mosquitoes, ticks, or fleas.

f. If any weapon not seeming to have an immediate casualty effect.

70. How to Protect Yourself During A Biological Agent Attack

a. Your first action for protection during a biological agent attack must be defense against breathing the biological aerosol. Your protective mask will give you complete protection from inhaling the biological aerosol. Know the conditions for masking without order or alarm (para 71).

b. You must protect your skin from a biological aerosol by arranging your field clothing so that as much skin area is covered as possible. Your clothing should be completely buttoned, and the trouser legs should be tucked into your boots. Covering the skin will reduce the possibility of the agent entering your body through cuts and scratches and also will prevent disease vectors from reaching the skin.

c. You should use insect repellents and insecticides as directed. Ordinary repellents and insecticides are effective against most disease vectors.

71. Conditions for Masking Without Order or Alarm

Automatic masking is necessary once biological operations have been initiated or information is available that they are about to be initiated, just as it is upon the threat of chemical operations. You will mask without order or alarm every time any one of the conditions shown in figure 8 occurs, and you must wear your mask until told to unmask. Study figure 8; remember the conditions for masking and what to do when an attack is suspected.

Section III. THINGS TO DO AFTER A BIOLOGICAL ATTACK

72. Biological Agent Detection

a. There is no simple method of detecting biological aerosol agents, since they are tiny particles of living matter so small they can be seen only under a microscope. You cannot see, feel, taste, or smell the microorganisms spread in a biological attack. If biological agents are known to be present, you will be informed and told what additional defensive measures you should take.

b. Even though biological agents are hard to detect, you must do what you can to alert your unit of an attack at the earliest possible moment. Every clue counts. A prompt report of suspicious clues or activities may lead to the prevention of many cases of illness, and may prevent deaths. You should inform your unit leaders or medical personnel of any illness you or your buddies have. Report at once any food or water suspected of making you ill.

c. Identification of a biological agent may require from several days to several weeks. Laboratory analysis of samples from infected personnel or animals or from the field must be made or symptoms of infected personnel or animals studied for positive identification of the agent.

73. How to Protect Yourself Against Biological Agents

There are several measures that will minimize the effects of a biological attack. These measures are summarized in figure 11. The most important ones are proper and timely use of protective equipment and decontamination.

a. Guard Against Contamination (fig. 10). Do this by avoiding food and water that could be contaminated and by using soap and water generously. Microorganisms can enter your body in food and water as well as in the air you breathe. Make it a fast rule to never eat any food nor drink any water unless you know that it has been checked and declared safe. Following a suspected biological attack, food from sealed containers can be eaten if the containers are boiled or washed thoroughly before the seal is broken. If biological agents have collected on your hands, you may spread some of them to your mouth or to your food. Guard cigarettes by keeping the package closed; take care not to contaminate the tip placed in your mouth.

b. Wear a Complete Uniform. If biological agents are disseminated by vectors, the agent can be passed on to you by the bites of the vectors. If you notice an unexplained or suspicious increase in the number of possible vectors, body covering is of great importance. All the body covering you

PRECAUTIONARY MEASURES FOR AVOIDING BIOLOGICAL AGENT CONTAMINATION

DON'T---

1. CONSUME NATIVE OR CIVILIAN FOOD OR DRINK OF ANY KIND. EAT AND DRINK ONLY APPROVED FOOD AND WATER.

2. PUT ANYTHING IN YOUR MOUTH UNLESS YOU ARE CERTAIN IT IS NOT CONTAMINATED.

3. BATHE IN LAKES OR PONDS.

4. TOUCH ANIMALS.

5. TAKE SOUVENIRS.

DO---

1. KEEP IMMUNIZATIONS CURRENT AND USE PRESCRIBED MEDICATIONS

2. BE ABLE TO RECOGNIZE THE BIOLOGICAL CONTAMINATION MARKER. KNOW WHAT IT MEANS.

Figure 10. Precautionary measures for avoiding biological agent contamination.

can get with field clothing is very desirable. All buttons should be buttoned. Trouser legs should be firmly secured by tying them down with extra shoelaces, then securing boots in the normal manner. Use extra shoelaces to firmly tie cuffs of jacket or shirt sleeves at the wrists. Use insect repellents and insect powders as instructed.

c. *Continue High Standards of Sanitation and Hygiene.* Remember that if you do not practice good personal cleanliness and proper sanitation measures, you are increasing your chances of becoming a disease casualty. Continuing high standards of sanitation and personal hygiene after the attack will help strengthen your own natural body defenses against disease.

74. Decontamination

a. If you suspect that you have been exposed to a biological agent, thoroughly scrub your face and hands as soon as the mission permits; use plenty of soap. Also brush your teeth and gums. As soon as the tactical situation permits, take a complete shower using plenty of warm water and soap. Clothing believed to be contaminated should be decontaminated at the first opportunity by boiling or by washing in hot soapy water. Your protective mask can also be decontaminated by washing in warm soapy water after removing the filter elements.

b. If you are told that a biological attack has occurred, you must be doubly careful of what you eat and drink. Food and water are the natural homes of many disease producers. Eating contaminated food and drinking contaminated water are sure ways of getting biological agents into your body. If contamination is suspected, you can decontaminate individual food supplies by boiling unopened cans in water for at least 15 minutes or by thoroughly washing them in soap and water or a disinfectant before breaking the seal on the cans. Water which has been boiled for at least 15 minutes is safe to drink in an emergency. You, as an individual soldier, should not try any other food or water decontamination procedures. Leave these measures to inspecting personnel and unit leaders; then eat or drink only those supplies which you know have been approved for your consumption.

c. You should wear your mask in a contaminated area until decontamination has been accomplished, either by personnel or through natural processes. Leaving your nose or mouth unprotected in a contaminated area may result in your becoming a casualty.

75. Treatment for Biological Agent Casualties

If you have ever had measles or a similar disease, you will remember that you were not sure just when or where you were exposed to the disease. Several days after you were exposed you began to feel sick, and then the other symptoms followed. Diseases caused by biological agents appear in much the same way—a few days to weeks after contact with the agent. For this reason, there is no first aid for biological agent casualties. You have taken immunizations for some diseases, and you may be given others. If you get a disease from a biological agent, you will be treated in accordance with the kind of disease you have.

76. Protective Measures Against A Biological Agent Attack

(fig. 11)

a. Report Sickness Promtly. If you or your buddies get sick, notify your leader or your unit medical personnel immediately. This will enable them to begin treatment and take additional preventive measures to minimize the effects of a possible biological attack.

b. Keep Yourself and Your Living Area Clean. Biological agents have trouble living in clean places. If you keep yourself and your living area clean, you help prevent the spread of disease, regardless of the source. In the field, strict personal hygiene and sanitation measures are absolutely necessary.

c. Take Prescribed Immunizations and Medications. Even though some immunizations may be overcome by large doses of biological agents, preventive medical measures are a valuable part of biological defense. Such measures are valuable only if you follow instructions.

d. Use Equipment and Clothing Properly. Take good care of your protective mask, keep it readily available, and put it on promptly when the need arises. Use your field uniform for maximum body covering.

e. Keep Your Food and Water Protected. Bot-

PROTECTIVE MEASURES	
1. HEALTH	Guard your health by good diet, sleep, and exercise A clean body and sanitary living area help prevent the spread of disease, regardless of its source
2. SHOTS	Keep your immunizations up to date as they increase your body resistance to disease and may prevent your becoming a casualty
3. PURITY	Eat and drink from only approved sources The enemy may try to contaminate food and water Contaminated food or water can cause sickness or death
4. REPORT	Be alert. Report suspicious activities that indicate the enemy may be employing biological agents Report sickness to unit leader or to medical personnel.
5. COVER	Microorganisms must enter your body to cause disease Your protective mask and clothing properly worn will protect you
6. AVOID	Avoid contaminated areas You help the enemy if you catch and spread disease
7. SCRUB	Scrub hands and face with soap and water frequently Take a complete bath as often as possible
8. STERILIZE	Clothing should be either boiled, scrubbed with soap and water, dry-cleaned, or aired in the sun
9. RUMORS	Remember your training Spreading rumors may cause panic Don't alarm others by repeating or exaggerating what you hear

YOUR MASK IS YOUR FIRST LINE OF DEFENSE AGAINST BIOLOGICAL AGENTS TAKE CARE OF IT!

Figure 11. Summary of protective measures against a biological attack.

tled or canned foods on which seals have not been broken are safe after a biological agent attack if the outside of the container is decontaminated before the seal is broken. Any food or water in the open will be contaminated and should not be consumed.

f. Keep Alert To Any Signs of Biological Agent Attack. Such clues as new or unusual types of shells or bombs, smokes of unknown nature, possible vectors, or any weapon that does not have an immediate casualty effect should be reported to your unit leader immediately.

g. Kill the Rumors. Defense is possible if you follow the simple rules given in this manual. Spread of disease from person to person is not likely; the effects of a biological agent attack normally will be confined to those directly exposed to the agent. Ignorance breeds fear. You and your buddies must know the facts concerning biological operations. Talk of biological superweapons is nonsense if you know the actual capabilities and limitations of biological agents.

77. Reporting

A seemingly unimportant bit of information concerning biological operations may actually be a valuable link in gaining intelligence on biological capabilities of the enemy. Information that you can collect and should report to your unit leader includes such things as—

a. Time of suspected attack.

b. Place of suspected attack.

c. Extent of the attack (if you can determine it).

d. Method used to release the agent.

e. Any effects produced.

78. Marking of Contaminated Areas

An area known to be or suspected of being contaminated with a biological agent should be marked so that you and others will be alerted to the dangers of biological contamination (para 10*d*). The standard biological marker is illustrated in figure 2. The triangular marker is blue on both sides, and the letters BIO in red are on the side facing away from the contamination. The name of the agent (if known) and the date and time of detection will be placed on the back of the marker. Study this marker and remember it. Do not enter areas that are marked with it unless ordered to do so. Biologically contaminated areas may not be marked, so you should always be alert to the possibility of biological contamination.

CHAPTER 4
PROCEDURES IN NUCLEAR WARFARE

Section I. THINGS TO DO BEFORE A NUCLEAR ATTACK

79. General

Nuclear warfare is warfare in which nuclear weapons as well as the conventional weapons of war are used. As you read this chapter, you will find that many of the things you do to protect yourself from conventional weapons will also give you protection from the effects of nuclear weapons. This chapter will give you a general understanding of the effects of nuclear weapons so that you will be able to protect yourself and continue your mission in a nuclear war. If you are interested in learning more about the effects of nuclear weapons, consult DA Pam 39–3.

80. How the Enemy Can Attack You

There are several ways by which the enemy can deliver nuclear weapons: artillery shells, aerial bombs, rockets, and guided missiles, and atomic demolition charges. Also, it is possible that an enemy agent might use a special nuclear device for sabotage.

81. Nature of Nuclear Explosions

a. A nuclear weapon is another means of causing an explosion. The heat and blast effects of a nuclear explosion are similar to those of a high-explosive weapon, but are greatly magnified. Nuclear radiation is the only completely different effect a nuclear explosion produces that other types of explosions do not produce.

b. An important difference between a nuclear attack and a large-scale high-explosive attack is the time involved. A high-explosive attack destroys buildings and kills people, but such an attack may last from several minutes to hours. However, an attack with a nuclear weapon strikes a large area at once, and the destruction occurs within a matter of seconds. While you may be given some warning of a coming air or artillery attack, and there may be time for you to take cover, there probably will be no warning of a nuclear attack. Therefore, it is essential that you are always alert and well prepared for a nuclear attack and that you know what to do at the moment of attack, during, and after the attack.

82. Effects of Nuclear Explosions

You have already read that a nuclear explosion produces blast, heat, and nuclear radiation effects. What, exactly, are the nature and extent of these effects?

a. Blast. The blast effect of a nuclear explosion is caused by the rapid expansion of the fireball, compressing the air around it. As the fireball grows, a wall of compressed air is piled up around it like the peel on an orange. Then, as the fireball slows its rate of expansion, the "peel" of highly compressed air breaks away and begins to travel outward in all directions from the point of burst. This wall of highly compressed air is called the blast wave, and very high speed winds accompany the wave as it moves away from the point of burst at about the speed of sound. This wave collapses or damages buildings, uproots trees, and fills the air with flying and falling debris. About one-half the total energy of a nuclear explosion is in the form of blast.

b. Heat. The heat and light given off during a nuclear explosion are called thermal radiation. The fireball reaches temperatures hotter than those on the surface of the sun and emits great quantities of ultraviolet, infrared, and visible light rays. In the area of ground zero, wood and other flammable materials usually will be ignited. Nuclear weapons similar to those used in World War II can produce burns on the exposed skin of individuals out to a distance of 4 kilometers (2.5 miles) from the point of detonation. More powerful weapons now available may cause burns at much greater distances.

c. Nuclear Radiation. Nuclear weapons produce two kinds of radiation hazards: initial nuclear radiation and residual nuclear radiation (which includes fallout and neutron-induced radioactivity). Nuclear weapons can be detonated so that no militarily significant (casualty-producing) fallout results; however, militarily significant neutron-induced radioactivity may be produced in a small area around ground zero. Knowing when each type of nuclear radiation will or will not occur, however, is not nearly so important to you as is your general attitude toward nuclear radiation. True, nuclear radiation is a dangerous effect of nuclear weapons, but it is based on certain known laws of nature. It can be understood and explained, and you can protect yourself against it. Having a healthy respect for its possible dangers—not blind fear of them—is the best way you can obtain such protection. Following the use of nuclear weapons toward the end of World War II, many groundless rumors about nuclear radiation injuries spread rapidly. Today, however, we know that the two Japanese cities where the nuclear weapons were used have been rebuilt and are safe places in which to live. Crops grown in surrounding areas are safe to eat, and the people are healthy and normal. World War II nuclear bombs were exploded to make maximum use of blast and heat, rather than nuclear radiation. Nuclear weapons of today are made in a variety of yields. A height of burst may be chosen to obtain maximum heat effects, maximum blast effects, desired radiation effects, or a balanced combination of these effects. The resulting nuclear radiation will not necessarily be more hazardous than the other effects.

(1) *Initial nuclear radiation.* Initial radiation is the radiation given off during the first minute after the explosion of a nuclear weapon. Although it can kill, it lasts only a short time. In built-up areas, such as cities, initial nuclear radiation may not cause as many casualties as flash burns, secondary fires, collapsed build-

ings, and falling and flying debris will cause. However, in open areas, such as will be found in many tactical situations, a foxhole or other shelter may protect an individual from blast and heat effects but may not provide total protection from initial nuclear radiation. By the time the blast effects of a nuclear explosion are over, the danger from initial nuclear radiation has also passed.

(2) *Residual nuclear radiation.*

    (a) Residual nuclear radiation is that radiation which remains on or falls back to the surface of the earth after the explosion of a nuclear weapon. Not all nuclear explosions cause militarily significant amounts of residual radiation. The amount depends upon the kind of weapon, its yield, and the height at which it explodes. The major source of residual nuclear radiation is fallout. As the fireball from a near surface, surface, or subsurface nuclear burst rises into the atmosphere, great quantities of materials, such as dirt, stone, water, and dust particles, are sucked up from the ground or body of water into the cloud that forms following the explosion. Radioactive particles are trapped in or attach themselves to these materials. The heaviest particles fall back to earth around ground zero; and as the cloud drifts downwind, the lighter particles fall back to earth. Thus, ground zero and large areas downwind of the target area are contaminated by this fallout. Fallout is further discussed in paragraph 97.

(b) Certain air bursts result in what is referred to as neutron-induced radioactivity. This radioactivity results when free neutrons escaping from the explosion combine with nonradioactive materials, such as bomb fragments and soil, and make them radioactive. Neutron-induced radioactivity will be in the immediate area of ground zero and may remain a hazard for a considerable period of time. Because these "hot" (contaminated) areas could exist after any nuclear explosion, you should not move into or across an area that has been hit by a nuclear weapon until you are told to do so. Your unit will have equipment that will detect and measure even small amounts of nuclear radiation originating from fallout or from neutron-induced radioactivity. You will be warned when such nuclear radiation is present or expected.

83. Types of Nuclear Explosions

In general, nuclear bursts are referred to as air, surface, and subsurface bursts, depending upon where the explosion occurs. This distinction is important to you because where a nuclear weapon explodes determines to a large extent the amount and kind of damage it does.

a. Air Burst. An air burst is a nuclear explosion in which the fireball does not touch the ground. The greatest damage from this type of explosion is from blast and heat. The only type of nuclear radiation usually considered hazardous from an air burst is initial nuclear radiation. However, bursts near the ground will produce small areas of radioactive soil around ground zero of the explosion. This radiological contamination is called neutron-induced radiation. A kind of fallout can result from an air burst if a low-yield weapon is detonated during heavy rains or if the nuclear cloud passes through rain clouds farther downwind. This phenomenon is called "rainout."

b. Surface Burst. A surface burst is one in which the point of detonation is on or above the surface of the earth and the fireball is in contact with the earth. Damage from blast is less widespread, and damage from heat is somewhat less than from an air burst of the same yield; also, about the same amount of initial nuclear radiation is present. Residual nuclear radiation occurs as fallout in areas around and downwind of ground zero.

c. Subsurface Burst. A subsurface burst is one in which the center of the explosion is beneath the ground or under the surface of the water. Most of the blast effects occur as a ground or water shock wave; as a result, the blast effects in the ground zero area are much less severe than from a comparable air or surface burst. Because the fireball gives off most of its energy under the ground or water, there are no significant effects from heat or initial radiation. Similar to a surface burst, a subsurface burst may produce considerable fallout both around and downwind of ground zero.

84. Types of Injuries Caused

Nuclear weapons injure in three ways—

Blast injuries—largely mechanical injuries caused by flying debris, by falling buildings, or by individuals being picked up and thrown against objects or onto the ground; also, in rare cases, injuries caused directly by blast overpressures.

Flash and flame injuries—burns caused directly by heat from the fireball or by secondary fires that are usually started by blast effects (*b* below).

Nuclear radiation injuries—sickness or death caused by either initial or residual nuclear radiation.

Casualties, of course, may be caused by a combination of two or even all three of the above types of injuries. For example, an unprotected soldier may receive a broken arm from flying timber, be burned on his face and hands from heat, and may receive a sickness-producing dose of initial nuclear radiation.

a. Blast Injuries. Few injuries are caused directly by the blast of a nuclear explosion, as the human body can withstand pressures greater than those required to knock down strong buildings. Most injuries are caused as an indirect result of the blast; for example, from falling buildings, flying objects, and shattered glass. Also, individuals can be picked up by the high winds accompanying the blast wave and thrown against buildings, vehicles, or onto the ground.

b. Flash and Flame Injuries. It has been estimated that approximately 50 percent of the deaths that occurred from the nuclear bombings of Japan were caused by flash burns. Persons in the open within 4 kilometers (2.5 miles) of the bursts received painful flash burns on exposed skin of the face and arms. Other burn injuries were caused by fires started from short circuits, overturned stoves, and ignited fuel supplies. If you are looking directly toward the explosion, your eyes may be permanently damaged by the flash or light produced by the explosion. Temporary blindness (flash blindness), similar to that caused when the flash bulb of a camera goes off in your face, is more likely to occur. This blindness may last from 5 to 20 minutes, its duration being longer in darkness than in daylight. Do not be frightened. More important, do not move around or fire your weapon while you are temporarily blinded. You may be injured or may become a target for the enemy.

c. Nuclear Radiation Injuries. Overexposure to either initial or residual nuclear radiation can cause radiation sickness and possibly death. Initial nuclear radiation lasts for only 1 minute after the explosion. However, residual nuclear radiation can exist in dangerous amounts for hours or even weeks after an explosion. There are no immediate indications of overexposure to nuclear radiation; its effects on your body may not appear until a number of hours after overexposure.

85. Why Nuclear Radiation is Dangerous

a. You are constantly coming in contact with radiation. Cosmic rays from outer space bombard your body every hour of your life. Since these cosmic rays originate in outer space so far from the surface of the earth, and because they are thinned out by the earth's atmosphere, they reach you in only very small amounts. Each time you have an X-ray, a controlled amount of X-radiation passes through your body. This exposure to radiation is acceptable because the harm it may do to you is outweighed by the good that early diagnosis and treatment of disease can do. The length of each exposure to X-radiation is short and the total exposure is low. The longer you are exposed to a source of radiation, the larger the dose you receive. The degree of injury from radiation is a direct result of total time exposed and rate at which the exposure is received. These same dangers of *length and amount of exposure* exist with nuclear radiation. So long as you do not receive more than certain total amounts of nuclear radiation, you will not become ill. The rays from X-ray machines are safe in medical treatment *only* so long as they are carefully controlled to protect patients and technicians from overexposure. Likewise, you must learn to protect yourself from the nuclear radiation produced by a nuclear explosion. Common materials, such as earth, concrete, and armor plating, will reduce the amount of nuclear radiation which will penetrate your body, if these materials are between you and the radiation source. In addition, your unit will have instruments that will enable your commander to determine how much nuclear radiation is present.

b. To understand why nuclear radiation is dangerous, you must review a few facts of science. There are four types of nuclear radiation with which we are concerned here: alpha particles, beta particles, gamma rays, and neutrons. The alpha and beta particles travel at high speeds but have short ranges. Gamma radiation differs from alpha and beta radiation in that it is actually a ray of energy similar to a radio wave or an X-ray and thus can travel much farther than the alpha and beta particles. Neutrons can cause damage in much the same manner as gamma rays.

c. Any agent or material that gives off nuclear radiation, such as alpha particles, beta particles, or gamma rays, is said to be radioactive. The particles and rays are expelled with great force, but each type is different in its ability to penetrate. Alpha particles can be stopped by a thin piece of paper, by clothing, or by the skin. Most beta particles can be stopped by a 3-millimeter (⅛-inch) thickness of metal and, to some extent, by clothing. However, high-energy gamma rays and high-speed neutrons can pass through concrete or earth just as radio waves penetrate the walls of buildings to make your radio operate. Some of the gamma rays and neutrons are absorbed as they pass through concrete or earth, but others get through. How much nuclear radiation gets through depends to a large extent on the thickness and composition of the shield (fig. 12).

86. How Nuclear Radiation Affects Your Body

a. Nuclear radiation damages body cells. Excessive exposure results in what is referred to as radiation sickness. You should remember, however, that exposure to nuclear radiation does not

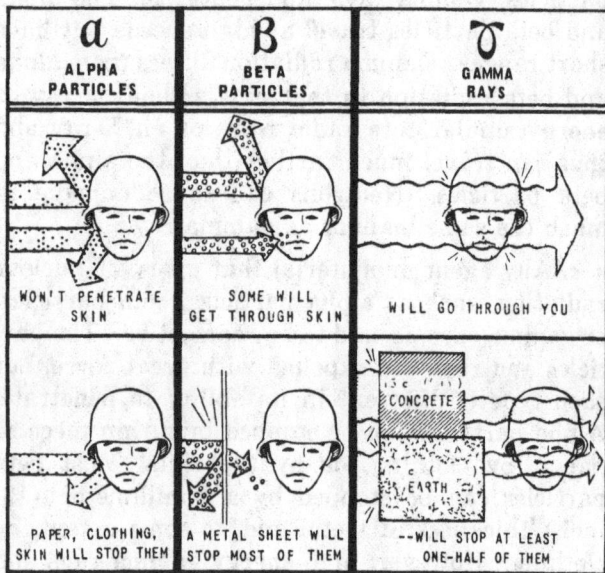

α ALPHA PARTICLES	β BETA PARTICLES	γ GAMMA RAYS
WON'T PENETRATE SKIN	SOME WILL GET THROUGH SKIN	WILL GO THROUGH YOU
PAPER, CLOTHING, SKIN WILL STOP THEM	A METAL SHEET WILL STOP MOST OF THEM	--WILL STOP AT LEAST ONE-HALF OF THEM

Figure 12. Types of nuclear radiation.

necessarily mean that you will have radiation sickness. The damage that nuclear radiation does to the human body depends on both the *amount* received and the *time* over which it is received. It takes a tremendous amount of nuclear radiation—either initial or residual—to harm you seriously. Thus, it is entirely possible for you to receive some exposure to either initial or residual nuclear radiation and suffer little or no effects. In fact, you receive radiation from natural sources during your entire lifetime and suffer no ill effects. The difference, then, is the amount of nuclear radiation you receive in a given time.

b. The effects of nuclear radiation are not noticed during exposure. You may receive an overexposure and feel perfectly well at first. If you receive enough nuclear radiation, such common symptoms as nausea, vomiting, and a weak feeling will occur within a few hours. Except in cases of extreme overexposure, these effects soon disappear. They may or may not occur again, depending upon the radiation dose received. If they do recur, it may be several days or even 2 or 3 weeks later. Personnel receiving a slight dose will recover quickly. *Those who receive a moderate dose may be ill for several weeks or months but will recover.* Only very heavy doses eventually result in death.

c. As you see, there are various degrees to which exposure to nuclear radiation can affect the body; more often the effects are minor or temporarily incapacitating rather than fatal. Bear in mind that you can have nausea, vomiting, and weakness from exposure to nuclear radiation without becoming completely incapacitated for duty. These effects do not mean that you require medical treatment or evacuation. You must continue your duties. If you later become incapacitated, you will be given the best medical care, and your chances of recovery are good.

87. Protective Equipment

a. *Clothing and Protective Covering.* Any type of clothing that covers you gives some protection against heat. Your clothing should, however, be loose fitting to provide dead air space between your body and the clothes. This air space acts as an insulator to give you better protection from the heat of the explosion. Keep your shirt on and the sleeves down. Whatever materials you can put between yourself and the fireball will be useful in stopping direct thermal radiation. For example, a shelter half, a blanket, or even a board will help. Your field clothing or shelter half or other protective cover will also keep radioactive dust particles (fallout) from falling directly on you and will thus make decontamination easier. Dust that does fall on outer clothing or on a cover can be removed by shaking the item in the wind or by brushing it with a broom made from twigs or limbs.

b. *Protecting Your Skin.* Beta particles may have a delayed effect on your skin. Although these particles will not penetrate very far into your body, they will damage your skin. It will become reddened and blistered. These indications may not appear until some time after exposure, so you may not know you have received skin burns until then. Correctly wear your regular field uniform or any protective clothing you are issued.

c. Protecting Your Hands. If so ordered, wear gloves to protect your hands if you enter a "hot" area. Later, when you wash your hands, it will be easier to decontaminate them if you have worn gloves.

88. Decontamination and First Aid

When the mission permits, decontaminate your body as described in paragraph 98. There are no first-aid measures for overexposure to nuclear radiation. First aid for injuries caused by heat and blast is discussed in paragraph 99.

89. Be Prepared

Alertness, self-discipline, and a readiness to obey orders quickly will prepare you to conduct yourself properly in nuclear warfare. Keep these principles always in mind:

a. When friendly forces use nuclear weapons—

  (1) Seek protection before the weapon is exploded.

  (2) Do not be so obvious in your preparation that the enemy realizes a weapon will be used.

  (3) Be prepared to attack aggressively to follow up the advantage gained.

b. When the enemy uses nuclear weapons—

  (1) Prepare defenses to reduce the weapon effects.

(2) Expect an enemy attack immediately after nuclear weapons are used and be prepared for it.

(3) Follow the direction of your leaders to continue the mission after the explosion. Take first-aid measures against heat or blast injuries if necessary, but do not let yourself forget the enemy.

Section II. THINGS TO DO DURING A NUCLEAR ATTACK

90. Your Mission

Your first duty is to carry out your mission. The many hours of training you have received have shown you the importance of respecting and obeying authority. Your own protection in a nuclear attack depends upon how well you work with your fellow soldiers in following the orders of your leaders. If your unit works as a team on the nuclear battlefield, you and it will get the best protection possible.

91. Protection

a. The important point to remember is that when a nuclear explosion occurs you do the same thing you would do if an HE shell exploded—*take cover*. If friendly forces are to explode a nuclear weapon where your unit would be exposed to its effects, you will be warned beforehand so that protective measures can be taken. However, an enemy nuclear attack will probably come without warning. Study figures 13 through 18 to learn the protection afforded by different shelters. Men

Figure 13. Walls are fair protection.

using any of the shelters shown in these illustrations stand a much better chance of escaping injury during a nuclear attack than completely unprotected men. Remember, in the open with no available shelter, a man who is flat on the ground is much better protected than a man who is standing. Therefore, if no shelter is immediately available, fall flat on the ground, preferably with your head away from the direction of the explosion, and cover your hands and face.

b. In a nuclear explosion, as in any explosion, the more material or distance there is between you and the burst, the safer you are. A foxhole gives

Figure 14. Hills are good protection.

better protection than a slit trench. A concrete
shelter gives better protection than a wood shelter.
The most important point to remember is that you
should make the most of whatever shelter you
have. Your training in protection against small
arms or artillery fire is also good training for protection against nuclear weapons. Your shelter
will work for you in these three ways: protect
you against flying debris, protect you against
burns, and cut down the amount of nuclear radiation that can get to you. If your shelter protects
you from the heat and blast effects of the explosion, it will also give you some protection against

Figure 15. Ditches are good protection.

the nuclear radiation (initial) that is given off immediately following the explosion. A well-constructed foxhole will greatly reduce the nuclear radiation dose you would receive in the open at the same location. The foxhole should be dug as deep as the situation permits, the deeper the better. You should crouch or get down as far as you can, at least 1 meter (about 3 feet) below the top, to obtain the maximum protection from your foxhole (fig. 17). A covered foxhole (fig. 18) provides much better protection than an open foxhole, particularly if the burst is over your po-

Figure 16. Culverts are excellent protection.

sition or is high enough so that the direct rays from the burst could reach the bottom of the foxhole. Timber covered with earth provides good cover; however, you should use anything you have available. Even a shelter half secured over the foxhole will provide some protection against thermal radiation (a poncho should not be used because it might melt and cause burns). The best protection, of course, would be obtained in deep underground fortifications. Learn the types of shelter and places that will give you protection from the effects of a nuclear explosion. Shelters

AGO 6631C

Figure 17. Deep foxholes are very good protection.

you would construct to protect against conventional artillery fire will also afford protection against nuclear bursts.

   c. Steel, as well as earth and concrete, gives protection against the effects of nuclear explosions. This protection is provided by tanks and armored personnel carriers and, to a lesser degree, by trucks. Personnel in an armored personnel carrier should remain in the vehicle, leaving it only when necessary or when better protection is immediately available. To provide better protection than the vehicle affords, the ground shelter should

Figure 18. Deep, covered foxholes are excellent protection.

be at least the equivalent of a 1.2-meter (4-foot) revetted foxhole with overhead cover. When under threat of nuclear attack, tank crew members should remain in their vehicle, leaving it only when absolutely necessary. In fact, tanks provide such good protection against the effects of a nuclear explosion that crews should seldom leave their vehicles to seek better protection. When hatches are locked, the armored vehicle gives excellent protection against both the thermal effects and the nuclear radiation from a nuclear explosion. Crew members under threat of nuclear attack should habitually wear helmets while in the vehicle and should keep all hatches locked. The amount of protection given by an armored vehicle depends upon the distance of the vehicle from the explosion, the yield of the weapon, and the height of the burst.

d. Most equipment is very vulnerable to the blast effects of a nuclear explosion. Just as digging in protects you, so it protects your equipment. Habitually dig in equipment and supplies to the maximum extent possible in a given situation. Their chances of being damaged are thus greatly reduced. Small, loose items of equipment, such as fuel cans, entrenching tools, rifles, and helmets, can be picked up by the blast wave and blown about with enough force to kill. If you are in an armored vehicle, insure that all equipment is removed from the interior of the vehicle or is secured. Radio antennas should be tied down. All combustible material should be removed from the outside of the vehicle and from its vicinity to prevent fires.

92. The Explosion

The first indication of a nuclear explosion will be an intense light, much brighter than sunlight. Almost immediately the well-known mushroom-shaped cloud will be formed. The ball of fire from the explosion rises fast, pulling with it a stem of dirt and debris. Heat comes with the intense light of the explosion, followed shortly by the powerful blast. Initial nuclear radiation is given off in the first minute after the explosion. If residual nuclear radiation results, it will be present in the ground zero area immediately following the explosion and will occur later in areas downwind of ground zero, depending upon the speed and direction of the winds through which the particles must pass during their fall to the ground. The damage a nuclear explosion does is determined by the yield of the weapon and the type of burst.

93. Act Fast

The most dangerous situation you may face is a nuclear explosion that comes without warning when you are in the open. You must think and act fast; every second is important and you must not waste time. You must automatically take action to minimize the effects of the explosion on your body (para 94a). The effects and the actions you must take are outlined in figure 19.

94. Protective Actions

The type of shelter available to you will depend upon your mission and location, whether or not you are warned, and many unforeseen factors.

a. If you are caught in the open and are not close enough to some shelter, drop flat on your stomach at once; close your eyes and protect your hands, neck, and face. DO NOT TAKE TIME TO DECIDE WHICH DIRECTION THE EXPLOSION IS IN, because if you delay you will be more likely to be injured by the blast and thermal effects of the explosion. If a ditch, culvert, or wall is close by, take cover there (figs. 13–16). DO NOT TRY TO GET TO YOUR FOXHOLE OR OTHER SHELTER if more than a

NUCLEAR ATTACK

ALWAYS STAY PROTECTED

(in underground shelters, basements, foxholes, tanks) when not required to be in the open.

DURING AND AFTER BURST	**TAKE COVER**	If you see a brilliant flash of light, DIVE FOR COVER or FALL FLAT on the ground, face down Protect head, eyes, and exposed skin Stay down until heavy objects stop falling.
	STAY CALM	Check weapon and equipment for damage. Contact your leader.
	CONTINUE MISSION	Be ready for further enemy attack. If fallout is expected, improve your position as situation permits. When fallout arrives, cover up and stay covered but alert until fallout stops

KNOW ALERT PROCEDURES FOR A FRIENDLY BURST. WHEN ALERTED, FOLLOW UNIT SOP.

Figure 19. Protection against a nuclear explosion.

NUCLEAR ATTACK

EFFECTS OF A NUCLEAR BURST

BLAST	**SHOCK WAVE**	Most injuries are caused by flying objects and individuals being hurled about by the high winds of the blast wave Keep down, stay in shelter
HEAT	**FLASH HEAT**	Bare skin can be burned at great distances from explosion Your clothes or any other material that will cast a shadow gives protection Cover exposed skin areas
HEAT	**FIRES**	Flash heat starts forest and brush fires Ignited fuel and short circuits start others Fight fires in the normal manner
RADIATION	**INITIAL**	Initial radiation occurs in the first minute after detonation By the time objects stop falling, this danger is over Good shielding will significantly reduce the extent to which you are affected by nuclear radiation
RADIATION	**RESIDUAL (FALLOUT)**	Fallout is insignificant from an air burst If it follows another kind of burst, you will be told what to do

Figure 19—Continued.

AGO 6631C

few steps away. Once in your shelter or on the ground, keep your eyes closed, get down as far as you can, and protect exposed parts of your body (figs. 17, 18) until the blast (bang) of the explosion passes. If you are inside a building, drop to the floor with your back to the window, or get under anything that will protect you—a table, desk, or counter.

b. If you are warned beforehand that a nuclear attack is expected, pick the strongest shelter you can get to in a hurry. Select one that is as firm and stationary as possible. A shelter which would normally stop heat or flying objects may be collapsed by the blast of the explosion. In the field, your foxhole, a ditch, or your armored vehicle probably will be your best protection against blast, heat, and nuclear radiation.

c. After you have taken shelter, stay where you are until heavy material has stopped falling. After about 90 seconds the greatest danger from the heat wave, the blast wave, initial nuclear radiation, and probably from falling debris will be over. Prepare to continue your mission. Your unit commander will have specially trained unit personnel to monitor for radiation hazards (fig. 20). He will then know whether residual nuclear radiation is present and, if so, the dose rate. He will decide how to accomplish the mission of the unit with the least amount of exposure to the radiation hazards.

Figure 20. Monitoring for radiological contamination.

Section III. THINGS TO DO AFTER A NUCLEAR ATTACK

95. Continue the Mission

a. After a nuclear weapon has been exploded, it would be dangerous for you to assume that the fighting is over. We, or the enemy, depending on which side uses the weapon, may follow up the nuclear attack with ground or airborne attacks. After a nuclear attack you must be prepared to attack, defend, or carry out other orders you may be given.

b. In order that the enemy can be taken by surprise, you may not be notified that a nuclear attack is to be made by friendly forces until only a few minutes before the weapon is to be used. An important technique in the employment of nuclear weapons on the battlefield may be to use the weapon on enemy frontline fortifications and emplacements. This may mean that the nuclear weapon will be employed close to your area. If it is, this is the moment that you must put into practice the training you have received in protection, shelter, and other nuclear warfare procedures. The more protective action *you* take, the better prepared you will be to attack if ordered while the enemy is still dazed from the nuclear weapon. It is necessary, then, for you to be able to protect yourself and your equipment if nuclear weapons are used by friendly forces and for you to be prepared to carry out your mission once these weapons have been used.

c. Just as you must be ready to follow up a nuclear attack on the enemy, you must also expect the enemy to do the same thing when he uses a nuclear weapon against you. It will be your responsibility to be prepared to defend yourself and your position against a possible enemy attack following a nuclear strike. Do not expect the enemy to limit himself to the nuclear weapon alone. You must be prepared to protect youself against non-nuclear weapons, including chemical and biological agents. Be ready to assume higher command positions if casualties in your unit make this necessary. The failure of an enemy attack will depend largely upon the alertness and ability of you and your unit to rally quickly following such an attack.

96. How Nuclear Radiation is Detected and Measured

a. Specially designed electronic instruments called radiac instruments are used to detect and measure nuclear radiation because it is invisible and cannot be detected by your five senses.

b. There are two types of radiac instruments: (1) dose-rate meters, used to locate radiological contamination and to measure the rate at which nuclear radiation is being absorbed, and (2) dosimeters, used to measure the total nuclear radiation dose received by an individual. Specially trained personnel of your unit will operate the dose-rate meters when the need arises. These instruments let your commanders know where nuclear radiation is present and the degree of contamination. This radiation is measured in *rad/hr*. Dosimeters will be worn by you or by a member of your squad or work detail when the need arises.

Very small, and resembling a fountain pen, the tactical dosimeter is clipped inside the jacket or shirt pocket and shows *how much* nuclear radiation an individual or a small group of individuals has received. This dose is measured in *rad* and is used as a basis for estimating an average dose for each member of the group.

c. It is the responsibility of your unit commander to have the unit area of interest or responsibility systematically checked for radioactivity. In this way, any radioactivity will be detected and dose rates measured. He then will direct the radiological defense measures to be followed by individuals working in or crossing the radiologically contaminated area. Follow these directives.

d. If you become separated from your unit, and are without radiac equipment of any kind, your primary concern will be to rejoin your unit, or any friendly unit, as soon as your mission permits. The real danger in this situation is exposing yourself to ionizing radiation without knowing it. If you observe a nuclear detonation, avoid the area where the detonation took place. If you observe what appears to be sand, dust, or ashes falling from the sky after seeing a nuclear detonation or for no apparent cause, assume that it is radioactive fallout and dig in quickly. Stay in shelter for at least 24 hours (longer, if you think you can still reach a friendly unit quickly), and then move toward friendly positions as rapidly as possible. If you come upon an area where there is a great deal of tree blowdown, alter your course toward friendly positions and avoid this area. The same holds true if you discover a large crater or an area of ground having a glassy appearance. Keep in mind that, without radiac equipment, you cannot tell when you are in a radiologically contaminated area.

e. Your unit commander will see to it that the firefighters, rescue workers, and soldiers who enter "hot" (contaminated) areas do not remain there long enough to be injured. You must not lose your head just because radioactivity is reported present. Remember, there is a lot of difference between *detectable* and *dangerous* amounts of nuclear radiation. For example, even the radiation from an ordinary luminous dial wristwatch will cause a roar in the earphones of one type of radiacmeter. The amount of nuclear radiation present is one of the factors that determines how long it is safe to remain in a contaminated area. Nuclear tests in which thousands of soldiers like yourself took part have proved that not all radioactive areas present a hazard to the soldier if he knows what to do.

97. Protection Against Fallout

You have already learned what fallout is. You know that this danger may come from a surface or subsurface nuclear burst, that it may be hazardous many hours after the explosion, and that it can be dangerous at considerable distances from ground zero. When you are in an area where there is danger of fallout, you should take the following actions (fig. 21):

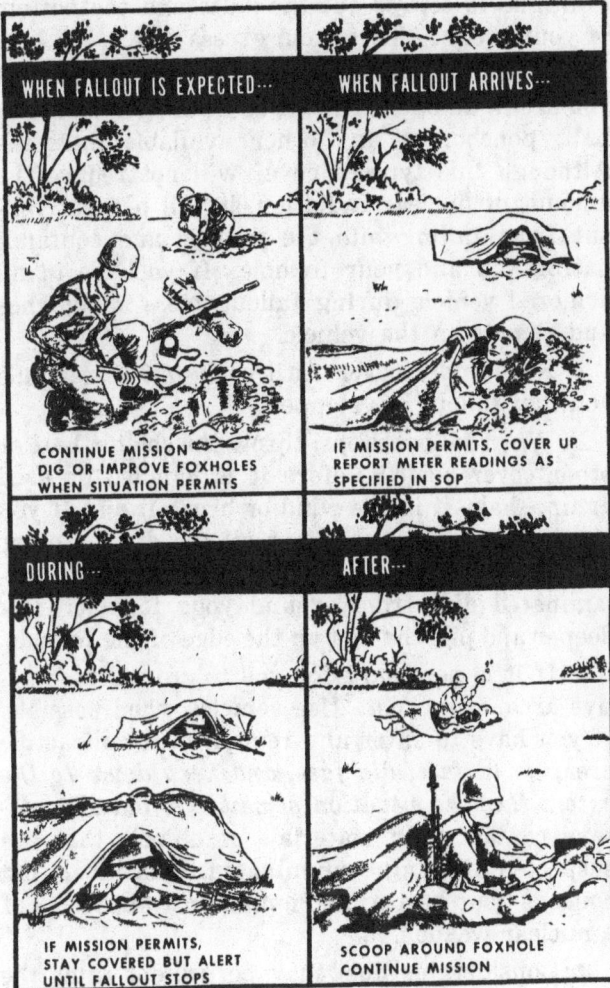

WHEN FALLOUT IS EXPECTED...

WHEN FALLOUT ARRIVES...

CONTINUE MISSION
DIG OR IMPROVE FOXHOLES
WHEN SITUATION PERMITS

IF MISSION PERMITS, COVER UP
REPORT METER READINGS AS
SPECIFIED IN SOP

DURING...

AFTER...

IF MISSION PERMITS,
STAY COVERED BUT ALERT
UNTIL FALLOUT STOPS

SCOOP AROUND FOXHOLE
CONTINUE MISSION

Figure 21. Protect yourself against fallout.

a. Dig a deep foxhole or other type of underground shelter and improve it as time permits. Continue to scrape out the sides and the bottom of your shelter. Throw out excess dirt.

b. When fallout begins, enter your shelter. If you are in an open foxhole, cover it with a shelter half, poncho, or any other available material. Although this type of cover will not reduce the amount of nuclear radiation, it will prevent fallout from falling into the foxhole and contaminating you and your foxhole. If you are in an armored vehicle during fallout, close all hatches and remain in the vehicle.

c. Keep under cover until your unit leader tells you that fallout has stopped.

d. When fallout stops, throw the shelter half or other cover aside. Before it is handled or used again, shake it in the wind or brush it off. If you are in a foxhole, scoop out all the dirt or other material which has fallen into it. Scrape contaminated dirt from around your foxhole. Dig deeper and pile the dirt on the edge of the foxhole.

e. If it is necessary for you to cross a radioactive area, *cross fast.* Use vehicles when possible. If you have to enter and remain in a radioactive area, *go in fast, dig fast, and keep down to the extent that the situation permits.* Avoid unnecessary contact with materials or objects that are suspected of being contaminated. Remember that *cover* is your best protection against all effects of a nuclear weapon.

f. Considerable dust may be present after the blast wave of the nuclear explosion has passed.

Any type of filtering device, such as a dust respirator, protective mask, or handkerchief held over the nose and mouth, will make breathing easier; however, it will not protect you from radioactivity.

g. As was mentioned before, you should take advantage of your clothing to prevent beta radiation injury to your skin. Correct wearing of your regular field clothing or any protective clothing you are issued will keep fallout particles from coming in direct contact with your skin, and by doing so, prevent beta radiation injury. If your exposed skin does become contaminated, follow the procedures for decontamination in paragraph 98.

98. Decontamination

a. If detection equipment shows that you are contaminated to a hazardous degree, you should decontaminate yourself as soon as the mission permits. You may be told to go to a personnel decontamination station or you may have to take a make-shift bath in your own area. Your outer clothing will serve as a trap for most radiological contamination. By taking off your clothes, you remove most of the contamination except what may be on exposed skin surfaces. Decontaminate your clothes by brushing off the dust. Then wash and rinse them thoroughly or set them aside to be sent to a laundry unit. You can decontaminate your weapon and personal equipment by wiping, brushing, or washing. You should decontaminate yourself as follows (fig. 22): Remove clothing and equipment. Take a shower or a bath if a

HOW TO REMOVE RADIOACTIVE PARTICLES FROM YOUR BODY

WHEN THE MISSION PERMITS ··

1 BRUSH OFF OR REMOVE AND SHAKE CLOTHING.

2 WASH WITH PARTICULAR CARE THE HAIRY PARTS OF YOUR BODY, BODY OPENINGS, AND BODY CREASES.

3 SCRUB YOUR HANDS AND NAILS.

4 SHOWER.

HAVE A MONITOR CHECK YOUR BODY FOR CONTAMINATION; IF NECESSARY, WASH AGAIN THOROUGHLY.

IF FREE OF CONTAMINATION, PUT ON CLEAN CLOTHING.

Figure 22. Decontamination of your body.

AGO 6631C

shower is not available, using plenty of soap and warm water. In washing, pay close attention to the hairy parts of your body, body openings, and body creases. Scrub your hands and nails thoroughly. After you have finished your shower, you should be monitored with a radiation detection instrument. If you are still contaminated, take another shower. If you are free from contamination, put on clean clothing.

b. Food and water can become contaminated by radioactive particles. Avoid using uncovered food or water if it is in a radioactive area. Canned food and covered water may be used with safety if the containers are cleaned thoroughly before being opened. Rely on trained personnel to check and declare harmless anything you put into your mouth.

c. If you are in a foxhole or bunker, after fallout has fallen in your area, scrape out a half inch or so of dirt around the walls of your foxhole and spread the soil over the ground around your position. This will get rid of the radioactive materials that have collected in your foxhole or bunker. Remember that considerable contamination can be kept out of your foxhole by use of overhead cover, such as a poncho.

99. First Aid

The first-aid rule in a nuclear attack is: Men help themselves and each other, as continuation of the mission permits.

a. In basic training you were taught the fundamentals of first aid for wounds caused by blast and heat. Knowing thoroughly the proper first aid may someday save your life or a buddy's life. First-aid measures for the wounds, fractures, or burns caused by the explosion of a nuclear weapon are the same as those for such injuries caused by nonnuclear weapons. FM 21–11 gives you details of the procedures needed for specific injuries caused by heat and blast. Learn these important fundamentals of first aid. When first aid is needed, take steps to stop the bleeding, clear the airway, protect the wound, and prevent or treat shock. Fast action in taking these vital first-aid measures can save lives.

b. There are no first-aid measures for nuclear radiation overexposure. As has been emphasized, the first indication that you have been overexposed to nuclear radiation probably will not appear until several hours after exposure. Then you may feel nauseated and begin to vomit. The time it takes these effects to appear depends on how much nuclear radiation you have received. You know, too, that nausea and vomiting can be caused by many ordinary battlefield conditions; alone, they do not indicate that you have been exposed to any nuclear radiation, much less to a harmful amount. So concentrate on continuing your mission and feel assured that medical personnel know what to do *if* and when you need treatment.

100. Reporting

The most important thing you can do after a nuclear burst is to continue your mission. The next most important thing you can do is to give your unit commander an accurate report of any burst you observe. The NBC 1 (Nuclear) report format provides that the following information be reported, if possible: the position of the observer, the azimuth from the observer's position to the burst, the time of attack, the location of the attack, and the type of burst. You may also take certain measurements, such as the illumination time, flash-to-bang time, nuclear burst cloud width, and nuclear burst cloud-top angle and cloud-bottom angle. You may become familiar with the methods for taking these measurements by reading FM 3–12. The information you give your unit commander will be evaluated and used to help him protect you from unnecessary exposure to radiation.

101. Marking of Contaminated Areas

Areas known to be radiologically contaminated should be marked with the standard contamination marker (para 10d). This marker is shown in figure 2; you should study the marker and be able to recognize it. The marker is white on both sides, and the word ATOM in black lettering is on the side facing away from the contamination. The dose rate, date and time of the dose-rate reading, and the date and time of the detonation that produced the contamination (if known) will be put on the back of the marker. The markers will be placed close enough together so that you will not miss them and enter a dangerous radiation area by mistake. However, remember that you may encounter contaminated areas that have not been marked, so remain alert to the possibility of radiological contamination. Your unit commander will have areas that are suspected of being contaminated checked with detection devices.

APPENDIX I
REFERENCES

AR 220–58	Organization and Training for Chemical, Biological, and Radiological Operations.
AR 320–5	Dictionary of United States Army Terms.
AR 320–50	Authorized Abbreviations and Brevity Codes.
FM 3–10	Employment of Chemical and Biological Agents.
FM 3–12	Operational Aspects of Radiological Defense.
FM 5–15	Field Fortifications.
FM 21–5	Military Training Management.
FM 21–6	Techniques of Military Instruction.
FM 21–11	First Aid for Soldiers.
FM 21–30	Military Symbols.
FM 21–40	Chemical, Biological, and Nuclear Defense.
FM 21–48	Chemical, Biological, and Radiological (CBR), and Nuclear Defense Training Exercises.
FM 21–75	Combat Training of the Individual Soldier and Patrolling.
TM 3–215	Military Chemistry and Chemical Agents.

TM 3-216	Military Biology and Biological Agents.
TM 3-220	Chemical, Biological, and Radiological (CBR) Decontamination.
TM 3-522-15	Mask, Protective, Field, M9 and Mask, Protective, Field, M9A1.
TM 3-4240-202-15	Organizational, DS, GS, and Depot Maintenance Manual: Mask, Protective, Field, ABC-M17.
TM 3-4240-219-15	Organizational, DS, GS, and Depot Maintenance Manual: Mask, Protective, Aircraft, M24.
TM 3-4240-221-15	Organizational, Field and Depot Maintenance Manual: Mask, Protective, Tank, ABC-M14A1, and Mask, Protective, Tank, M14.
TM 3-4240-223-15	Organizational, DS, GS, and Depot Maintenance Manual: Mask, Protective, Tank, ABC-M14A2.
TM 3-4240-255-14	Organizational, DS and GS Maintenance Manual: Mask, Protective, Tank, M25A1.
TM 5-311	Military Protective Construction (Nuclear Warfare and Chemical and Biological Operations).
TB 3-4230-207-10	Decontaminating and Reimpregnating Kit, Individual, M13.

DA Pam 39–3	The Effects of Nuclear Weapons.
ASubjScd 21–6	Individual Protective Measures for Chemical and Biological Operations and Nuclear Warfare.
GTA 3–1–2	CBR Decontaminants.
GTA 3–4–1	Field Protective Mask M17.
GTA 3–4–2	Individual Protection from Fallout.
GTA 3–4–3	Defense Against CBR Attack.
GTA 3–7	CBR Duties of a Gas Sentinel.
GTA 3–7–2	Things to do Under Nuclear, Biological, or Chemical Attack.
GTA 3–20	Field Protective Mask, M9A1.
MF 20–7815	The Effects of Atomic Bomb Explosions.
MF 20–7956	Atomic Support for the Soldier.
TF 3–1860	Individual and Unit Decontamination of Toxic Chemical Agents.
TF 3–2651	Effects of Mustard Gas on Individuals.
TF 3–2652	Individual Protection Procedures Against Mustard Gas.
TF 3–2653	Protective Mask Fitting—Part III.
TF 3–2654	Protective Mask Inspection—Part IV.
TF 3–2661	Use of Field Impregnation Sets.
TF 3–2809	CBR Protective Shelters—Part I—Field Shelters.
TF 3–2871	Decontaminating Procedures for Toxic Chemical Agents.

TF 3–2977	CBR Protective Shelters—Part II—Semi-permanent and Permanent Shelters.
TF 3–3033	Employment of Toxic Chemical Agents—Part I—Offense.
TF 3–3034	Employment of Toxic Chemical Agents—Part II—Defense.
TF 3–3036	CBR Permeable Protective Outfit—Part I—Donning Procedure.
TF 3–3037	CBR Permeable Protective Outfit — Part II — Removal Procedure.
TF 3–3055	CBR Duties of Sentinels.
TF 3–3133	Use of CS in Training.
TF 3–3139	Nuclear Yield Estimation, Field Expedient Methods.
TF 3–3203	Protective Mask Fitting and Drill (M17).
TF 3–3204	Protective Mask Inspection (M17).
TF 20–2531	Individual Protection Against Atomic Attack.
Standardization Agreement 2002	Marking of Contaminated or Dangerous Land Areas.
Standardization Agreement 2004	Toxic Alarm Systems.
Standardization Agreement 2047	Emergency Warnings of Hazards or Attacks.

APPENDIX II
STANDARDS OF INDIVIDUAL PROFICIENCY

1. Objective

The objective of the standards of individual proficiency is to train the soldier to properly perform individual protective procedures to minimize the effects of a chemical, biological or nuclear attack so that he will be able to assist his unit to accomplish its mission.

2. Standards

The standards of individual proficiency are that you must be able to—

a. Properly don and check your protective mask within *9 seconds* following an alarm or recognition of a chemical or biological attack.

b. Recognize, by appearance or effects, the existence of a chemical hazard and take protective action.

c. Recognize chemical, biological, or nuclear attack; methods of delivery; and alarms; and take appropriate protective action.

d. Perform simple decontamination of yourself, your clothing, your personal equipment, your individual weapon and position, or your crew-served weapon.

e. Perform first aid for injuries caused by nuclear weapons and chemical agents.

f. Recognize all standard markers that indicate areas contaminated with chemical agents, biological agents, or radioactive material.

g. Cross or bypass contaminated areas with minimum danger to yourself.

h. Maintain individual protective equipment.

i. Perform your mission during employment of chemical, biological, or nuclear weapons by either friendly or enemy forces.

j. Consistent with your mission, take protective measures against the blast, heat, and nuclear radiation effects of nuclear explosions.

3. Measurement of Individual Proficiency

The proficiency of your performance of the actions listed in paragraph 2 must be measured under the most realistic training conditions practicable. Your proficiency will be measured by an individual CBR proficiency test similar to those in FM 21–48 and Army Subject Schedule 21–6.

APPENDIX III

THE ABC–M17 FIELD PROTECTIVE MASK

Section I. MASK INSPECTION AND FITTING

1. General

Procedures for inspection and fitting of the ABC–M17 field protective mask are given in paragraphs 2 through 4 below. Pertinent references are TM 3–4240–202–15 and GTA 3–4–1. TM 3–4240–202–15 gives specific instructions for cold-weather use of the mask and for firing the rifle when wearing the mask.

2. Formal Inspection

a. When field equipment is not displayed, the command is PREPARE FOR MASK INSPECTION. The unit opens ranks as prescribed in drill regulations. Each soldier masks and checks for proper fit and adjustment as the inspecting officer approaches. The mask is then removed and handed to the officer, who examines it for cleanliness and condition. The mask is then handed back to the soldier, who replaces it in the carrier. Its position is checked by the officer.

b. When field equipment is displayed, protective masks are examined after displays have been inspected.

Caution. Masks should not be displayed on the ground in bright sunlight for lengthy periods.

The unit commander gives the command: PROTECTIVE MASKS WILL BE INSPECTED. Subordinate commanders order SIDE CARRY—SLING CARRIERS. This command is executed and inspection then follows the procedures outlined in *a* above.

3. Informal Inspection

You are responsible for the condition of your mask. You must inspect the mask when you receive it and periodically thereafter to detect defects. In addition, *supervised inspection* is conducted by the unit commander or someone designated by him. Inspection procedures are as follows:

a. Carrier. Remove mask from carrier and examine carrier. Check for mildew, stain, holes or tears, broken or torn straps, bent or missing D-rings, broken hook snaps, broken snap fasteners, frays in stitching, and for torn or missing belt-carry strap. Points where deficiencies are most likely to occur are circled in figure 23. Mask accessories that are authorized to be stored in the carrier must be in the correct positions (TM 3–4240–202–15 and para 21). *Unauthorized items must be kept out of the carrier.*

b. Filter Element Assembly. Check the filter element assemblies for damaged filter elements or incorrect position in cheek pouches, nosecup flap improperly located behind chin stop, flaps incorrectly buttoned, and for water damage. (Water destroys the efficiency of filter elements.)

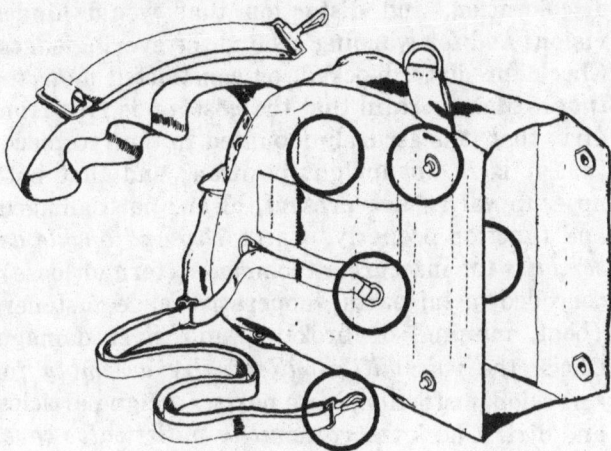

Figure 23. Inspection of mask carrier.

c. *Facepiece.* Check facepiece for holes, tears, or splits; for tackiness, hardness, or brittleness; for dirt or mold; and for fine cracks (dry rot). Check for permanent set that might affect the fit. Inside of facepiece must be free of foreign particles that might fall into the outlet valve and interfere with its functioning. Pay careful attention to the *eyerings;* check eyerings for corrosion or damage. Stretch rubber around eyerings to make certain there are no holes and that each eyering is properly crimped around the eyelens. Check eyelens for cracks; for defects, such as chips, scratches, discoloration, and distortion that would hinder vision; and for warping around the eyering edges. Check for dirty, blocked, or constricted *deflector tubes*. Make certain that the *nosecup* is free from dirt; that it is securely mounted to the facepiece; that it is in an upright position; and that both nosecup valves are present, clean, not damaged, and function properly. Check *clip and buckle assemblies* for insecure attachments (torn or loose), corroded metal parts, inoperative slide fasteners (bent, missing, or broken), and rivet damage. Check the *voicemitter-outlet valve assembly* for corrosion, distortion, loose parts, foreign particles, and dirt. Check the *voicemitter-outlet valve cover* for cracks, tears, breaks, stiffness, or distortion. Check the *outlet valve* for foreign matter and improper seating of valve disk. Check the *cheek pouches* for dirt, foreign matter, and presence of both flap buttons. Check the *inlet valve assemblies* for broken or damaged cap, flocked surface of cap dirty or clogged, damaged inlet valve seat, valve disks not in place on studs, and damaged inlet valve disks. Check the *faceblank* for loss of temple pins.

d. Head Harness Assembly. Make certain that the head harness assembly is free from any defects that would make correct adjustment impossible. Check for torn or frayed straps, loss of elasticity of straps, and mildewed webbing. (Head harness may lose its elasticity through improper storage, or rubber threads of the elastic straps may break if head harness is worn very tight.

Clinch tips should be tight.) Check the functioning of the head harness assembly; put on the mask, and adjust each strap by pulling out the loose end to see if the strap can be tightened easily. If all straps cannot be adjusted in this manner, the head harness should be replaced.

4. Adjusting Fit of Mask

This procedure is conducted informally under the direction of the unit commander or his representative. (For further information on adjusting fit of mask, see TM 3-4240-202-15.) Steps for adjusting fit of the mask are as follows:

a. Loosen the head harness straps sufficiently to allow easy positioning of the mask on the face. Hold the mask by the voicemitter-outlet valve assembly firmly against the chin with one hand and center the head harness pad on the back of the head with the other hand ((1), fig. 24).

b. Hold the head harness pad firmly against the head with one hand; remove hand from the voicemitter-outlet valve assembly and alternately tighten the two top straps (forehead straps) just enough to remove any slack. (Straps are best adjusted by a quick jerk or pull rather than by a steady pull.) Similarly, tighten the two bottom straps (check straps) to attain a comfortable fit (moderately tight).

Caution. Do not remove your hand from the head harness pad while adjusting forehead and cheek straps.

c. Remove hand from head harness pad; using both hands, tighten middle straps (temple straps) simultaneously to moderate and equal tightness. (Buckles should be flat, and straps should clear ears and fit comfortably.)

d. Make sure that facepiece fits smoothly around your face. To check for an airtight fit, shut off air inlet on each side of facepiece with palms of hands, inhale *normally*, and hold breath for 10 seconds ((2), fig. 24). Repeated adjustment of straps may be necessary if facepiece does not give an airtight fit. However, straps should not be too tight; headaches and discomfort may result or a channel (gap) may develop at the edge of the facepiece, allowing agents to enter. If leakage persists after careful efforts for adjustment, the mask does not fit and should be repaired or re-

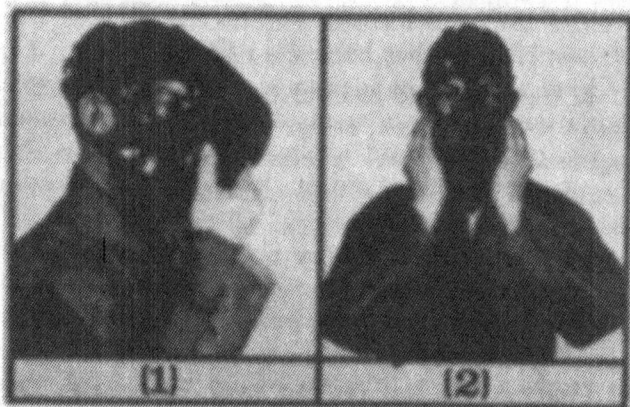

Figure 24. Adjusting fit of the mask.

placed. A larger or smaller size should be tried. If mask is too large, the eyes will be below the center of the eyepiece; if mask is too small, the eyes will be above the center of the eyepiece (TM 3–4240–202–15).

Section II. CARRYING POSITIONS AND MASK DRILL

5. Carrying Positions

There are five basic carrying positions (fig. 25) for the ABC–M17 mask—

a. Side carry.

b. Front carry.

c. Back carry.

d. Leg carry.

e. Belt carry.

6. How to Assume the Carrying Positions

a. Side Carry Position (fig. 25). The following steps are taken for assuming the side carry position.

(1) Hold carrier waist high in left hand by short strap with D-ring, carrier flap toward the body.

(2) Grasp shoulder strap near snap with right hand.

(3) Pass shoulder strap outside the left elbow to back. Shoulder strap should not be twisted, but should be laid flat and smooth around shoulder.

(4) Bring shoulder strap over right shoulder and fasten snap to D-ring. Adjust strap

so that distance between armpit and top edge of carrier is width of hand.

(5) Place carrier securely against body. Fasten body strap around waist so that carrier fits snugly.

(6) Assume final side carry position.

b. *Front and Back Carry Positions* (fig. 25). These positions are assumed by rotating the carrier from the side carry position.

c. *Leg Carry Position* (fig. 25). The following steps are taken for assuming the leg carry position.

(1) Hold carrier waist high in left hand by short strap with D-ring, carrier flap toward the body.

(2) Swing carrier to left side, slightly to rear; reach behind back with right hand and grasp shoulder strap.

(3) Bring shoulder strap around waist, and fasten snap to D-ring.

(4) Adjust body strap around leg, and thread snap through D-ring.

(5) Return body strap to rear of leg; fasten snap to D-ring in rear of carrier.

(6) Assume final leg carry position.

d. *Belt Carry Position* (fig. 25). The belt carry position utilizes a 5-inch strap of cotton webbing sewed horizontally across the back of the carrier. Two loops enable the attachment of the carrier to two metal keepers on the belt.

SIDE CARRY

Figure 25. Carrying positions for the ABC–M17 mask.

FRONT CARRY

Figure 25—Continued.

146

AGO 6681C

BACK CARRY

Figure 25—Continued.

LEG CARRY

Figure 25—Continued.

BELT CARRY

Figure 25—Continued.

7. Procedure for Drill

The six commands and actions which make up the mask drill are illustrated in figure 26.

AT THE COMMAND

"GAS"

STOP BREATHING

Remove headgear with right hand
and open carrier with left hand.
Place headgear as directed.

1a

Figure 26. Mask drill, ABC–M17 mask.

Hold carrier open with left hand;
grasp facepiece just below eyepieces
and remove mask with right hand.

1b
Figure 26—Continued.

Grasp facepiece with both hands,
sliding thumbs up inside facepiece
under lower head harness straps.
Place other fingers straight and
together outside facepiece above
eyepiece. Lift chin slightly.

1c
Figure 26—Continued.

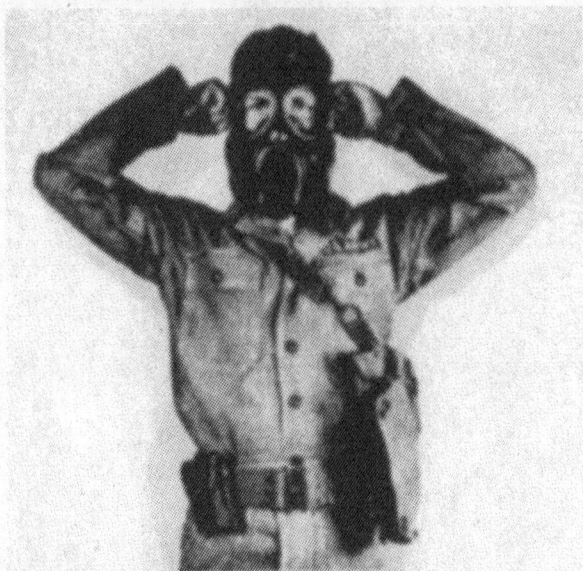

AT THE COMMAND

"PLACE"

Seat chin pocket of facepiece firmly
on chin. Bring head harness smoothly
over head, insuring that head harness
straps are straight and head pad is
centered.

2a
Figure 26—Continued.

Smooth edges of facepiece on face
with upward and backward motion
of hands, pressing out all bulges to
secure airtight seal.

2b
Figure 26—Continued.

AT THE COMMAND
"CHECK"

Close outlet valve by cupping heel of right hand firmly over opening; blow hard to clear agent from facepiece.

Figure 26—Continued.

Block air inlet valve assemblies,
shutting off air supply. Inhale.
The facepiece will collapse if
there are no leaks. (If wearing
cotton gloves, see para. 24b(7).)

RESUME
BREATHING

Figure 86—Continued.

AT THE COMMAND

"COVER"

Replace headgear.
Fasten carrier flap.

Figure 25—Continued.

AT THE COMMAND

"REMOVE MASK"

Remove headgear with left hand.
With right hand grasp facepiece
by voicemitter-outlet valve
assembly and remove facepiece
with circular motion (downward,
outward, upward).

5a

Figure 26—Continued.

Replace headgear. With left hand
fold head harness into facepiece;
then open carrier. Holding carrier
open with left hand and holding
facepiece below eyepieces, start
mask toward carrier with chin
pocket first and eyepieces facing
downward.

5b

Figure 26—Continued.

AT THE COMMAND
"REPLACE MASK"

Insert mask into carrier, tilting mask upward so that facepiece is facing out.

Figure 26—Continued.

Close carrier flap.

6b
Figure 26—Continued.

Section III. DISPOSITION OF HEADGEAR, WEAPON, AND EYEGLASSES

8. Disposition of Headgear and Weapon While Mask is Being Donned

a. During drill, the instructor may direct the placement of headgear and weapon (if carried). When the helmet is worn, if the chin strap is fastened, the helmet may be placed on the left arm; if the chin strap is not fastened, the helmet (or helmet liner) may be placed between the knees or over the canteen carrier. The rifle is left on if carried at "sling arms"; otherwise, it is placed between the knees, and the helmet or helmet liner may be hung on the rifle.

b. During a chemical or biological attack, it is important to mask quickly and, when time permits, to secure the helmet, weapon, and other equipment. Care should be taken to prevent your rifle and other equipment from becoming contaminated.

c. A quick means of removal of the helmet when chin strap is fastened is to place the left hand on the forehead under the front of the helmet and quickly tip it forward off the head, allowing it to slip by the chin strap over the left arm.

9. Disposition of Eyeglasses While Mask is Being Donned

a. During drill, the instructor may direct the disposition of personal eyeglasses.

b. In combat, eyeglasses should be equipped with an adapter to prevent loss of the glasses while donning the mask.

(1) The adapter can be made from elastic cord or nonelastic material, such as shoestring, and attached to the temple pieces of the spectacles ((1), fig. 27).

(2) Before donning the mask, the spectacles are dropped so that the adapter is around the neck and glasses hang over the chest ((2), fig. 27). The protective mask can be donned without interference by the glasses, and the glasses will not be lost ((3), fig. 27).

(3) At a convenient time after donning the mask, the glasses and adapter can be transferred to a pocket or other suitable site.

Figure 27. Use of eyeglass adapter while donning the mask.

INDEX